To Speak, to Tell You?

POEMS

Sabine Sicaud
1913-1928

INTRODUCTION & NOTES

Odile Ayral-Clause

ENGLISH VERSIONS

Norman R. Shapiro

Black Widow Press is an imprint of Commonwealth Books, Inc., Boston, MA. Distributed to the trade by NBN (National Book Network) throughout North America, Canada, and the U.K. All Black Widow Press books are printed on acid-free paper. Black Widow Press and its logo are registered trademarks of Commonwealth Books, Inc.

Joseph S. Phillips, Publisher
www.blackwidowpress.com

Cover Design: Kerrie Kemperman
Text Design: Sue Knopf of graffolio
Cover Illustration: © Vallentin Vassileff | Dreamstime.com

ISBN-13: 978-0-9818088-8-8

Library of Congress Cataloging-in-Publication Data on file

Printed by BookMobile

10 9 8 7 6 5 4 3 2 1

To the memory
of Marguerite Fechner
O. A.–C.

❧

To the memory
of Joseph McMahon
N. R. S.

Our sincere thanks go to the people who contributed to the making of this book: to Marguerite Fechner and Georgette Converset for sharing many memories of their days at La Solitude; to Armelle Danysz-Millepierres, daughter of François Millepierres, for her enthusiastic support of our project; to the Schreiber family, present owners of La Solitude, for their warm welcome; to the librarians of the Agen library for being especially helpful.

We are also happy to express our gratitude to Lawrence Ferlinghetti, John Hollander, Robert Sabatier, and Richard Wilbur for their kind support and appreciation of our work.

Finally, our warmest thanks to Jacques Barchilon, the friend who brought us together and thus originated our collaboration on this work.

Publication of this book has been aided by a grant from the Thomas and Catharine McMahon Fund of Wesleyan University, established through the generosity of the late Joseph McMahon, and by a grant from the College of Liberal Arts at California Polytechnic State University, San Luis Obispo.

CONTENTS

PATHS

ILLNESS

PREFACE

Translating Sabine Sicaud has been a labor of love. Then again, translating any poet is, for me at least, always such to some extent. To spend the time and expend the spiritual energy required to bring over into another life a poet's creation certainly demands an identification with her or him that is little short of intellectual love. In Sabine's case, compassion adds another dimension. The pity—"akin to love"—that one feels for this anguished Wunderkind could not help but intensify that identification; that attempt to get into her skin, her mind, her soul, and to transpose the ideas, images, joys, and, no less, the physical and emotional pains that are the stuff of her remarkable poetry.

I think, without waxing overly philosophical, that such a spiritual identification is what one always tries to accomplish as a translator of poetry. And, of course, to do so while respecting the original and without letting one's own artistic personality cloud or—worse—transform it.

One would think that to identify with a child poet would be particularly difficult for the mature translator. (Chronologically mature, at least.) But Sabine made the task of "getting into her skin" much easier than it would be with any ordinary children. Her adult intelligence, her broad knowledge of a world with which she had had precious little actual experience; the clarity of her ideas and the precocity of her vocabulary; her familiarity with the traditions of French poetry even when she chose not to observe them to the letter... Everything about her work has invited the translator into a collaboration with a poet well beyond her years. A joyful collaboration, notwithstanding the searing sadness that many—too many—of her poems evoke.

When Odile Ayral-Clause suggested the possibility of a modest collection of Sabine's poems I was already somewhat familiar with her work, having included a handful of translations in a volume of French women poets then in preparation. The "modest collection" soon became the present virtually complete œuvre. One never knows (or loves) a poet so well as when one plays the translator, delving into a body of art and making it temporarily one's own. I am grateful to my collaborator for giving me that opportunity.

A few words are in order to explain some of the technical and aesthetic problems that Sabine's work has posed. Since her original manuscripts no doubt passed through several pairs of hands on their way to eventual publication, traditional format was not always observed. Some poems were printed with differing line lengths and indents reflecting varying syllable-count; others, not. Often these disparities looked seemingly capricious. In the interest of consistency, we have decided to do away with indents entirely, while still respecting overall format, especially where it seems organic to the sense. On the other hand, we follow Sabine's—or whoever's—lower case beginnings of mid-sentence lines in a number of poems; and only in a few cases do we "correct" obvious errors.

In matters of French prosody, Sabine's generous use of the sacrosanct alexandrine, the decasyllable, and other syllabic lines, has begged a certain regularity, but certainly not a slavish one-for-one imitation, which would be an exercise in futile virtuosity corresponding to no poetic need. Only rarely do I use the 12-syllable line that Pope wanted categorically to ban from English verse. Where Sabine modifies her verse's metrical constraints, or frees it entirely, I try to follow her lead. As for rhyme too, she uses it or not, as she sees fit, and rarely in a set formal pattern. I do likewise. And if my versions occasionally sound a little starchy for the mouth of an eleven/fifteen-year-old, I ask the reader to remember that Sabine was home-schooled by super-erudite parents surrounded by other no-less-erudite adults, and that her French vocabulary belies her own tender years. Her childhood world was anything but childish.

It is possible, I suppose, that, had she lived, Sabine might have been tempted to revise her poems entirely, or at least retouch them, in order to bring them more into line with traditional French norms. I would hope not. As they stand, they are a splendid expression of "freed" verse: a midpoint between the total formlessness of *vers libre* and a poetry that respectfully tips its hat, in passing, to the constraints of earlier poetic "rules"; a verse *à la* the likes of a Jacques Prévert of a generation later. I hope my versions bring across that constrained freedom that stands out as one of her hallmarks.

Norman R. Shapiro

INTRODUCTION

Those who knew Sabine Sicaud, the precocious author of an exquisite collection of poems published when she was only thirteen, called her "le petit elfe" [the little elf]. She had blond braids that reached down to her waist, a hint of mischievousness in her smile, and luminous blue eyes. There was indeed something subtly magical in her playful intelligence and in the fervent compassion she manifested for all things small and vulnerable. But Sabine too was vulnerable. Stricken with a painful illness, she died at the age of fifteen, in 1928. During the last year of her life, confined to her bed, the young adolescent expressed her suffering in poems unforgettable in their poignancy, powerful imagery, and depth of vision.

A true poet, not merely a child prodigy, Sabine had reached an amazing intellectual maturity nurtured by the bountiful environment in which she lived and deepened by her struggle with suffering. In his anthology of twentieth-century French poetry, prominent writer Robert Sabatier attested to the poetic genius with which Sabine created "a poetry that is real and ripe like a young fruit." Sabatier, like others before him, wondered what would have happened to "the little poet, the great poet Sabine Sicaud if she had lived."[1] While the answer to this question belongs to the realm of dreams, the poems Sabine left behind paint a world thoroughly rooted in reality. Sabine's is the voice of a sensitive child attentive to nature's most fragile creations, and of an impassioned adolescent whose haunting images reveal the extent of her suffering. But it is also the cheerful voice of a happy young girl determined "to see and know everything,"[2] a girl who loved and understood life more fully than many of her elders.

Sabine was born on 23 February 1913 in *La Solitude,* her mother's childhood home. Built on the outskirts of Villeneuve-sur-Lot, a picturesque town in southwestern France, *La Solitude* was enclosed by a large iron gate, which opened on a long alley lined with century-old plane trees, forming what Sabine called "a green cathedral."[3] Beyond the alley lay an inviting park where exotic sequoias, magnolias, cedars, and palm trees flourished alongside more humble native plants. A pond, hidden among this exuberance, provided a peaceful environment for a refreshing interlude, and a mysterious grotto lured visitors wishing to meditate. The ivy-covered country house, with its two turrets, stood at the end of the alley. Sabine describes her world in a long poem dedicated to *La Solitude,* as a verdant refuge of trees, cacti, and ivy. She repeats the word "green", sings it, and embroiders it with a variety of qualifiers. Tender or somber, emerald or lime, green adorns the cedar as it does the frogs in the pond—a green world and a nurturing "island refuge."[4]

Sabine's brother Claude, two years her senior, shared his sister's boundless affection for this green kingdom. For the children, *La Solitude* was both a beloved home and an inspiring teacher. Sabine and Claude did not attend one of the local public schools but, instead, received private tutoring in the humanities and the arts. At the same time they were given the freedom to pursue their own interests, the opportunity to explore nature, and the intellectual incentive to read the books in their parents' extensive library, rich in Greek, Latin, and European classics. Their liberal education emphasized discovery rather than the strict curriculum typical of French education at the time. Marguerite Ginet-Sicaud, Sabine's mother, later conceded in a letter to a friend that their education may have been the object of fair criticism, yet she added wisely that as many paths lead to learning as to ignorance. "I don't know," she wondered, reverting to the term of endearment long used for Sabine, "where Minouchka learned drawing, music, and all that she knew though she did not show it."[5]

This somewhat mysterious comment tends to overlook the influence of the children's "remarkable" tutor.[6] He must have been the same one who taught elements of drawing and music to Sabine and, along with the Sicauds themselves, the one who guided her readings. Sabine's poetry alludes to Greek and Roman mythology as well as classic tales routinely taught to French children: Tales from *A Thousand and One Nights,* Alphonse Daudet's *Letters From My Windmill,* La Fontaine's fables, etc. More importantly, references to Dante, Shakespeare, and Cervantes point to very challenging readings for someone who was not yet in her teens.

Sabine enjoyed reading and writing in winter, when cold wind and grey skies made outdoor exploration uncomfortable. As soon as spring exploded with new life, she turned to "the magic book" offered by *La Solitude.* This book did not simply recount the story of the seasons, it brought it to life. There, the child saw spring's first leaves, stretching out their "little fingers" toward her, in defiance of the burning sun, the goat, and the caterpillar.[7] Later she encountered the cedar, the oak, and the elm, clothed in their rich summer leaves. And when, in autumn, the ivy colored the walls of the old manor a blazing red, Sabine watched how her "books"—the leaves of the plane tree—transformed themselves into blond and rich brown leather bindings, and perched like birds on the branches of the old plane tree. *La Solitude* itself was the richest book of all, an inexhaustible source of knowledge that nurtured the most precious qualities encountered in childhood: imagination, spontaneity, and inquisitiveness—qualities that remain intact

in Sabine's poetry. Out in the garden, the young poet observed
an ever changing world and mused:

> . . . can there be any living things
> More alive than a garden—ever blooming,
> Lush and mysterious, obstinate, perfuming
> The air, so full of creatures living there
> That we chat with a thousand genies, looming—
> Aladdin-like—from who knows how or where?[8]

The Sicauds often said in jest that it must have been one
of these little genies that dictated poems to their daughter, an
observation not far from the truth when one considers that
the young poet found her inspiration through a direct contact
with nature.

Sabine was only six when she began scribbling little poems
in the medical brochures discarded by her doctor-grandfather.
In his anthology of French poetry, Louis Vaunois recounts
how the girl would tip-toe toward her mother and ask:
"Would you like me to read you another poem?" Later, she
asked how verses were written, so her mother gave her classic
poetry to read. She found it "rococo." Her mother then gave
her contemporary poetry, but she found it "obscure."[9] Guided
by her mother and her teacher, Sabine learned about prosody,
but she kept her own voice. Despite her youth, her writing,
even then, displayed an unusual bond with the living world
that surrounded her, a bond reflected in an anecdote fondly
recalled by her mother. Having spotted her daughter perched
on a cedar branch, Madame Ginet-Sicaud walked toward the
tree. Sabine firmly stopped her. "Don't bother me," she said, "I
am with the cedar."[10]

As she grew older, Sabine routinely filled up notebooks
with thoughts—hers and other people's. According to writer
Rose Celli, first approached to edit Sabine's poems after her

death, these were "written in a round, naïve, and firm writing: half a page or three lines, or three words."[11] For years, the notebooks, kept in a basket that had housed the family dog, were easily accessible to visitors. After Madame Ginet-Sicaud's death, Suzanne, the long-time caretaker, was granted the right to spend the remainder of her days in *La Solitude,* and to oversee its belongings.[12] On several occasions, François Millepierres, a friend of the family and the editor of Sabine's posthumous poems, begged Suzanne to give him the basket, but she stubbornly refused. Eventually, the precious archives that could have shed more light on the upbringing of the child-poet, and her literary interests, disappeared, and their fate remains uncertain. As can be expected, the few anecdotes recorded in local newspapers provided scant information on the poet's creative routine. In one anecdote, pestered by a journalist who wanted to know where such a young girl had learned to write poetry, Sabine answered: "At home, at *La Solitude,* in my parents' big garden. I observe the life of animals and things." As the journalist, not to be put off, persisted and asked if she liked other poets, she retorted: "No, except for a few, like Verhaeren and Rollinat. . . ."[13]

Although neither poet left any discernible influence on Sabine's own highly original work, this perhaps offhand answer to a bothersome journalist indicates that Sabine had read at least some symbolist poetry. More celebrated in their own day than in ours, Verhaeren and Rollinat were on the fringes of the symbolist movement and not nearly as visible as the likes of a Rimbaud, a Verlaine, or a Mallarmé—poets who took esthetic pleasure in breaking down the syntax and form of French verse's traditional alexandrines, freeing the poetic language from its constraints. The child poet may well owe to the symbolists the freedom and skill with which she handled the complexities of French versification; yet it is not surprising, given her age, that her "natural talent" would remain untouched by their exploration of the metaphysical and mystical realm of poetic symbols.

Sabine Sicaud lived at a time when French poetry was moving away from specific schools and movements. The symbolist "revolution" was over and the surrealist movement was in its infancy. During this period, tired of the purely cerebral universe that dominated later symbolist poetry, many poets returned to a direct expression of feelings, often focusing on the observation of the natural world and on personal commentary on life—an approach long cherished especially by women writers. After centuries of subservience, women finally started to make strides in all areas, including poetry, and the beginning of the twentieth century is marked, in France as in English-speaking countries, by the blossoming of poetry written by women. Unlike their English and American counterparts—one thinks of Muriel Rukeyser, born in the same year as Sabine, or Elizabeth Bishop, born two years earlier, as examples—French women were not able to follow in the footsteps of important female models like Amy Lowell, H.D., or Marianne Moore, for instance, and their contribution to the French literature of the period is not as substantial as those of English-speaking women poets. Nevertheless, it is visible. Whether they viewed nature as a constant source of wonder and extolled the charms of their native country, or whether they sang maternal love, meditated on the cycles of life, and even dared to celebrate lesbian passion, women like Anna de Noailles, Lucie Delarue-Mardrus, Cécile Sauvage, Gerard d'Houville, and Renée Vivien were among the most prominent poets of this period. Anna de Noailles, especially, triumphed with *Le Cœur innombrable* in 1901, and was elected as the first female member of the Royal Academy of Belgium and the first to be made a commander of the Legion of Honor, though even her celebrity could not, at that time, gain her entrance into the all-male Académie Française. It was not until 1980 that novelist

Marguerite Yourcenar was to achieve the prestige of being the first woman accepted into that venerable institution.

The possibility of this type of recognition must have been far from the mind of child-poet Sabine Sicaud, but it is safe to assume that she was aware of the new visibility enjoyed by women poets, thanks to her friendship with Anna de Noailles. Besides, it is not at all unlikely that Sabine's mother, herself an exceptional woman, would have placed examples of women's poetry into her daughter's hands.

In her youth, Marguerite Ginet-Sicaud, a petite and charismatic woman, was thought to bear some resemblance to the actress Sarah Bernhardt. Her children called her "Filliou"— a term of endearment given to her by her mother—and her husband called her "Amrita"—a Buddhist expression meaning "immortal." But to her friends, she was the very incarnation of *La Solitude*. She completely identified with the place where she had enjoyed a happy childhood and, later, she tried to recreate the same environment for her children. Exceptionally well-read, endowed with a brilliant intelligence and a keen sense of observation, Madame Ginet-Sicaud had spent a few early years working as a journalist in Paris. Yet she could not long remain away from her roots and, after marrying Gaston Sicaud, she returned permanently to her home in Villeneuve. Far from being isolated in the provincial town or limited by its size, this captivating woman attracted a wide coterie of intellectuals who would make the trip to Villeneuve solely for the pleasure of spending a few hours in her engaging company. "By a miracle I never really understood," Marguerite Fechner, a close friend of the family, remembered in a letter, "though she rarely left her home, she always knew everything."[14]

Gaston Sicaud, Sabine's father, was a lawyer and a member of the City Council in Montauban, a nearby city lying south-east of Villeneuve. Nicknamed "Lama-père" for his love of Buddhism, he had a generous heart and an unquenchable passion for politics. A staunch socialist, he kept a regular correspondence with his long-time friend Jean Jaurès, the important socialist leader. It was only the latter's assassination in 1914 that put an end to their dialogues. For Gaston Sicaud, Ancient Greek and Roman orations constituted real poetry. He knew many of these orations by heart, in their original languages, and he took great pleasure in reciting entire discourses of Demosthenes within the resounding family grotto. His friendly booming voice could sometimes be overheard as he hiked through the countryside outside of Villeneuve. Returning home famished after an hour or two of exertion, he eagerly traded walking-stick and political reflection for a hearty bowl of soup, often surrounded by friends who would join the family for dinner. Marguerite Fechner remembered with nostalgia how everyone, both family and guests alike, would wash the dishes, start a fire in the fireplace, and warm the beds with oak embers. Huddled before the fireplace, they would conclude the evenings with impassioned discussions on the most esoteric of subjects as well as the most prosaic.[15]

Visitors who came to *La Solitude* took home with them exciting anecdotes and a wealth of ideas they had shared by the fireplace, weaving a sort of legend around the family. The Sicauds captivated many people with their effortless originality, unassuming generosity, and impressive learning. Naturally, the local population tended to view them as eccentric because of their unconventional way of life as well as their memorable ancestors. Everyone in Villeneuve knew the story of Dr. Malbec, Sabine's great-great-grandfather, who played the violin, wrote comedies in verse and prose, and taught ballet to female students at a local boarding school. Once, he traveled by foot all the way to Rome and earned his keep along the way by playing the violin. Finally, after turning eighty, Dr. Malbec stopped practicing medicine in order to study law at the university of Poitiers, where he became something of a celebrity.[16] For Sabine, who wanted "to see everything and know everything,"[17] Dr. Malbec provided a vivid example of a life full of happy surprises and realized dreams.

Though they remained attached to the great traditions of French humanism, the Sicauds were attracted to Buddhism and turned to vegetarianism at a time when both were viewed as strange habits for Europeans. They displayed the same kindness to animals as they did to human beings. Sabine's poems constantly allude to the animals who lived with them: Bouchut the cat, Dickette the dog, and Diégo the horse. Bouchut and Dickette went wherever they wished, while Diégo and the chickens freely roamed the park. Even the vegetation enjoyed complete freedom, left to grow on its own. The trees were never pruned—not even the plane trees. A universal brotherhood prevailed at *La Solitude,* a brotherhood from which the young poet drew her vision of the world.

When she was eleven, Sabine submitted her poem "Le Petit Cèpe," or "The Little Mushroom" to the *Jasmin d'Argent,* an annual literary contest still held in Agen to this day, and conducted, for the sake of impartiality, under conditions of strict anonymity. The jury unanimously awarded her poem a silver medal.

Like most of Sabine's early poetry, "Le Petit Cèpe" reflects a playful but sensitive observation of plants and animals, and expresses compassion for their fragility. The little mushroom opens his umbrella to shelter lady bugs, is used as a table by the frogs, and contributes to the profusion of colors displayed by spring. Personified as a being in his own right, he leads an innocent and simple life, in complete harmony with his surroundings. Sabine speaks to him directly and weaves a tale around him without losing her sense of humor. Warning the mushroom against "big feet" and "frying pans", she quips that she won't be an ogre for her tiny playmate. The undeniable charm of this poem stems from its immediacy and directness, and from the opportunity it offers readers to enter the world of a child. Irregular meter and rhyme convey a sense of freedom, and enjambments interlacing through lines of six, eight, ten, or twelve syllables, impart an exuberant, expansive feeling of discovery before the wonders of life.

When writer Marcel Prévost, president of the jury, and member of the Académie française, discovered that the author of the poem was an eleven-year-old girl, he found himself in a predicament. It seemed impossible that a child could construct a scene so skillfully or handle French versification with so much ease, much less demonstrate a surprising knowledge of botany. He suspected one of those literary hoaxes not foreign to French letters. At the same time, Prévost recognized the fresh new voice of this poem as one of youth. No adult would think of fretting so over a mushroom, except to put it in a frying pan. Neither would an adult recognize in this tiny creature a brother in need of protection, with a unique and fragile life of its own. The president of the jury could not eliminate a poem of such quality without proof of deception. Besides, he wanted to meet this enigmatic young girl; he decided to settle the matter himself.

Thus Prévost invited Sabine and her mother to his home and, pointing to his black cat, Fafou, whose dark silhouette stood out against the whitewashed wall, asked Sabine to write a poem about her. Leaving the girl alone at a writing table, he took Madame Ginet-Sicaud on a long tour of his garden. When they returned after an hour or two, the new poem, although quite different from "Le Petit Cèpe," proved to be no less skillful and imaginative. Playing on the devilish reputation of black cats, on the one hand, and the house pet's gentle familiarity on the other, Sabine lent a disturbing dualism to "Fafou." The improvised result, at times echoing the disquieting world of Rollinat, perfectly blends sensitive observation with fantastic dream.

At the award ceremony, Prévost, elated by his discovery, spoke at length about the child he called "the star attraction of the contest." "Her piece is of an exceptional quality," he said, "to the extent that we feared a hoax, believing that an adult poet hid behind the pleasant façade of this charming contestant. The inquiry proved that the poem was authentic and sincere." At this point, Prévost almost let his enthusiasm get the better of him. "How can I express the pleasure I personally feel at this revelation of a true poetic talent, new, rich, luscious, perfectly original? Verses that resemble no others, that recall no reading, that are truly themselves, at last... at last!"[18]

The year following her success at the *Jasmin d'Argent,* Sabine won other prizes at the *Jeux Floraux de France,* the most prestigious French literary contest, including the grand prize for "Autumn Morning." A century earlier, another very young French poet named Victor Hugo had won prizes in similar contests, but the great Hugo was to wait until he was twenty to see his first book of poetry, *Les Odes,* published. Sabine, on the contrary, was only thirteen when, in 1926, *Les Cahiers de France* collected and published twenty-nine of her poems under the title *Poèmes d'enfant,* or "Childhood Poems." Anna de Noailles, who presided at the *Jeux Floraux de France,* wrote the collection's preface, noting with admiration that "nature and life are offered to us by this child with extraordinary talent and generosity."[19]

When they were children, Jane Austen and Virginia Woolf also produced various pieces of writing. Their imaginary world imitated and often subtly criticized the adult world they observed daily. Other very young writers chose more visible forms of rebellion. In "Les Poètes de sept ans," for example, Arthur Rimbaud reveals how, as a seven-year old boy, he used dreams to escape from the dreariness of his daily life, though later, he would turn to outright anger and derision. Sabine, on the other hand, lived in a remarkably harmonious environment.

Her imaginary world, where grown-ups are barely present, does not strive to mirror the real world of *La Solitude,* let alone rebel against it; instead, it effortlessly connects to it and revels in it.

Most of the works included in *Poèmes d'enfant* describe Sabine's immediate surroundings. She is moved by the sad fate of the sweet chestnut, astonished by the crimson purple of an exotic heather, and attentive before the naked limbs of the tamarisk in winter. In "Autumn Morning," the poet uncovers such abundance of life in the church's small garden that the reader longs to linger there even as the bell calls for mass. Like other children, Sabine marvels at the most simple things, but her curiosity is compelled by a deep sympathy for any young and fragile being. In her eyes, the mushroom and the chestnut, the laburnum and the tamarisk exude intense vitality. The chestnut conceals a heart beneath its shell, laid open by the knife that stabs it, and the mushroom lies hidden from the men who seek it. Yet Sabine also recognizes this fragility as the very essence of the life cycle. The laburnum, which appeared dead in winter, revives "with sunshine hair," gilding the landscape, while the bare tamarisk with "fingers frail and small," blooms in a cloud of pink flowers. Beside them, evergreens lack inner grace, being impassive to the miraculous rite of the dawn of spring.

Although Sabine Sicaud was admired by Anna de Noailles, her vision of nature differs from that celebrated poet's. Like the romantic writers, Noailles often projects her own thoughts and emotions on the natural world. In Sabine's poetry, nature is observed for its own sake, with a delight and a sense of wonder also found in Colette, with whom Sabine has strong affinities. The young poet must have read *La Maison de Claudine,* a book published in 1922 and often given to adolescents. She would have found there a reflection of *La Solitude:* a nurturing island dominated by a wise and generous mother living in harmony with all the plants and animals she protected. Sabine and Colette share an attentive solicitude for anything that breathes and grows. Theirs is a physical world independent of abstraction, one to which they are wholly connected.

Though *La Solitude* was a safe haven, it remained open to the outside world. The Sicauds frequently harnessed their horse Diégo to the family cart for invigorating rides to the center of Villeneuve, taking the travelers across the thirteenth-century bridge adorned by the charming chapel of Notre-Dame-du-Bout-du-Pont. The three towers that once stood on the bridge had disappeared long since, though on the horizon two other towers could be seen: the Tour de Pujols and the Tour de Paris. Monsieur Sicaud knew the Tour de Pujols as a resting point along his favorite hike to the countryside, but Sabine only had eyes for the Tour de Paris because, near by, the owner of a coach company had turned his stables into a movie theater. The Père Desclos Company, royally renamed "The Palace," projected the silent films popular on both sides of the Atlantic.

Sabine adored cinema. She confided to a journalist that motion pictures were her passion, that she even much preferred them to reading poetry.[20] She subscribed to *Mon Ciné,* a cinema magazine and, after her success at the *Jasmin d'Argent,* her mother rewarded her with a visit to the magazine's headquarters in Paris. Sabine saw her dream of visiting a film studio realized when she was allowed to spend a whole afternoon in the Gaumont studios and watch the filming of *Le Puits de Jacob* [Jacob's Well]. It is said that she even began trying her hand at scriptwriting, though no examples have yet been found, nor are they likely to be.[21] Once, when she met an old man who did not understand the appeal of the curious new genre, she was so disconcerted that she wrote what may be the first poem to the glory of cinema. "Come to the narrow, gray-walled room, and sit there in the dark," she writes vividly, recreating a movie theater's ambiance: the darkness, warmth, and muffled sounds; the striking odor of barley sugar and toasted almonds wafting about; the dreams that, for a time, become reality. Using her pen like a magic lantern, Sabine evokes landscapes, actors, and well-known heroes with breathtaking mastery. Her fragmented descriptions simulate the sensual bombardment of the images bursting on the screen.

In Sabine's time, even more than today, when the film's escape has become routinely accepted, cinema offered an entrance into unfamiliar worlds. Sabine shared with her brother a love of faraway places and the allure of adventures and travel. Claude possessed an imaginative photographic memory that allowed him to recreate the atmosphere, the rhythm of life, and the local character of places he knew only through tourist guides. Sabine, not surprisingly, exploited her thirst for untravelled places through poetry. Possibly influenced by the exoticism then in vogue, sparked by poet and world-renowned traveler Valéry Larbaud, she began a series of poems often entitled "Chemins," or "Paths"—real paths weaving through the landscape, as well as inner paths that lead to peace, love, and God. Having long observed Diégo, the little black horse of La Solitude, she knew that he still carried within him the mystery of his homeland, the faraway Sierras. "His name, just like his race, comes from down there," she writes. His eyes, "gazing in surprise," hold memories and secrets he would never disclose. Perhaps because of Diégo, horses play an important role in Sabine's quest. In "Horses' Path," a strange white horse awaits her on an island; not the country horse of an actual childhood song recalled in the poem, but a symbolic one beckoning her toward freedom and adventure.

Often, Sabine's reveries emanate from an object and even a simple word. A postcard from abroad, the magical names of Florence, or Popocatepetl, the words "heart," "outlaw," or "moon," at times also conjure memories from past lives. During this period, Sabine, influenced by her parents' Buddhism, believed in reincarnation. Much later, Madame

Ginet-Sicaud told François Millepierres that her daughter's singular gifts must have arisen from a previous life, "from a memory preceding birth."[22] Sabine herself professed to believe that, in another life, she lived in Florence with her mother, grandmother, and great-grandmother. She remembered the Arno River and the garden filled with irises. Or perhaps she lived in Russia where everything "sings in 'a'"—Katia, Masha, Tania, niania, baba, isba—and where her horse came from Siberia. In the west, she recalled open spaces, the pampas, and, of course, the fascinating Indian name of Mount Popocatepetl. In the north, somewhere beyond Vancouver, she wore a fur coat, and her brothers hunted bears in icy caves. The "path" poems vibrate with the eagerness and charm of youthful travels. But, as Sabine notes in "Western Paths," while paths carry her around the globe, freedom lives fixed within her.

Within herself, Sabine encounters peace, love, and God. At first she looked for peace in the face of a baby, a blond-haired child, or an old woman; she scanned landscape paintings and listened to Mozart's music. Finally, she understood that peace is found in the most humble things—a cricket, a lamp's soft light, a fragrant breeze—when she took the time to notice. As for love, she knew it well; it enveloped her every day at *La Solitude*. Still, the heart's contradictions puzzled her. She wonders in "The Heartbreak Path" how the same heart can bear suffering and joy at the same time, how it can survive and renew itself. A wounded heart could not possibly experience all that life has to offer, she muses, nor could it be "Made new, or shun its endless destiny / From life to life, free of what it has sown." And she playfully concludes that she does, indeed, need several hearts.

For Sabine, there exist various paths to God. These paths can be smooth or rough, solitary or abounding with friends; they can cross deserts, mountains, oceans, and sometimes never even depart from home. They lead to a God of tolerance, wisdom, humility, and, especially, of compassion.

The compassion naïvely expressed by eleven-year-old Sabine for the little mushroom or the first leaves of spring, adopts a more somber, more dramatic tone two years later when the new adolescent becomes fully aware of the insidious presence of suffering around her. Within "the leafy loveliness" of the Gavaudun Valley, she shudders to discern traces of the miserable pariahs who, long before, cried out their pain from "The Lepers' Grotto." Through the legend of "The Old Woman in the Moon," she pities the weariness of a frail old woman bent under the burden of a firewood bundle. More poignantly, in "The Garden's Path" she endures the agony of a tree crucified by ruthless pruners, an agony that will soon become her own.

Like other girls her age, Sabine loved to swim in the Lot River when the summer heat grew stifling. One day in 1927, she cut her foot while bathing. Later, she complained of pain in her leg, but the local doctor could not find anything severely wrong with it. The mysterious illness spread into her other leg, then throughout her entire body. Since her skin showed neither festering nor dying tissue, it could not have been gangrene, yet an invasive and crippling pain gnawed silently at her bones.[23] Distraught, Madame Ginet-Sicaud arranged to have a well-known bone specialist travel from Bordeaux to examine her daughter, but he proved as puzzled as the doctor from Villeneuve. In those days, to be sure, medicine did not yet have the help of advanced technology and sophisticated drugs; thus the diagnosis of an illness rested solely upon the doctor's prior knowledge and experience. In prolonged and in-depth observation of the patient's symptoms lay the only possibility of diagnosis. The doctor therefore proposed to admit Sabine into his Bordeaux clinic for an indefinite length of time. But a new drama arose when Sabine adamantly refused to leave her beloved home. Unable to bear the heartrending pleadings of her daughter, Madame Ginet-Sicaud relented. They would not leave *La Solitude* for Bordeaux.

Considering medicine's limitations at the time, it is difficult to determine now whether or not this decision sealed Sabine's fate. In a letter written around 1954, Madame Ginet-Sicaud spoke of medical mistakes and described the tragic event as a very simple accident "that would not be serious today."[24] It seems likely in hindsight, that Sabine was suffering from osteomyelitis, a very painful illness that enters the blood stream through a skin wound and can be carried to the bones. Nowadays, osteomyelitis can be cured with antibiotics, but in 1927 it was still an illness that most physicians could neither diagnose nor treat. Only a highly-skilled surgeon could have performed an operation to expose the bone and clean it out, removing the infected tissues. Even so, this procedure offered no guarantee that the patient would be cured.

At the *Jasmin d'Argent* three years earlier, Marcel Prévost had expressed his enthusiasm for Sabine's poem but also his concerns over future influences, difficult to control at her impressionable age. Three years later, these same words, colored by the unexpected tragedy, ring with a bitter irony. "The danger," he had pointed out, "is the young age of the poet... What impact will these years until she is twenty have on her? The readings? The literary friendships?" Then, switching to a lighter tone he had added in jest: "Under the Ancien Régime, I would have tried to have her temporarily locked up in the Bastille—treating her, of course, as gently as possible. Oh well! It's in God's hands!"[25]

In God's hands... For the child-poet, maturity of thought leapt past influences; it arrived, with unforeseen brutality, through confrontation with her deadly illness. The radiant child who spoke to the cedar and befriended the little mushroom now lay shut inside a melancholy room, while her disconsolate mother watched over her day and night. There, Sabine waged a lopsided battle against "the invisible beast with tiny teeth" which tore at her relentlessly. There, she transcribed the raw experience of inexorable suffering and impending death in truthful, even violently candid poems.

Sabine's painful terminal illness turned the vibrant kingdom of *La Solitude* into a drab, desolate world occasionally visited by incompetent doctors. As she observed them without indulgence, Sabine regained her sense of humor: "What harm these sad-faced doctors will have done me," she writes in "Doctors." She contrasts their ignorance to the wisdom of Bouchut, a cat who chews grasses when he is sick and successfully treats himself. Sometimes, she dreams of the ideal doctor, handsome as a god, young, and full of life. Like a magician, he would restore hope, health, and joy to her life. Then, remembering that the doctors who visit her are far from this ideal model, she wishes for her ideal's opposite. Let him be feeble and ugly as a scarecrow and so old that, by comparison, she could believe in her own vigor and longevity.

Unfortunately, wit could not chase away the most visible symptoms of her illness, her fever and pain. Fever arrived in waves to sap the strength of her fragile body, burn her cheeks, parch her lips, and leave her wasted and raving in her bed. In "Fever Days," her delirium transforms her thirst into a fantastic vision where the desired water evanesces into images of fog, morning dew or snow, dancing on the ceiling and knocking at her window. But hers, the unquenchable thirst of the desert sands, cannot be appeased.

Worse still was the poet's suffering during that interminable winter. Sabine "screamed with pain as soon as she was touched; so as not to provoke such inhumane pain, her parents did not change or bathe her. When relatives or friends had the opportunity to provide the necessary care, it always ended in a drama for the child and her mother... "[26]

"Pain, I Abhor You" rails one vehement address to the gruesome enemy who mercilessly torments the poet. This dramatic poem is also a response to *The Honor of Suffering*, a volume of poetry published by Anna de Noailles, who, now aged, mourned the loss of her youth and the death of dear friends. The chasm separating the older poet from the younger, raked by physical pain and facing an untimely death, could not grow wider. Tortured in her flesh, Sabine knows that physical suffering offers no redemption, and she resentfully derides the older poet's belief. Her impassioned address aims at a personified Pain upon whom she heaps insults. She describes her as "a tiny-toothed, biting beast," a criminal bent on destruction, a horrible witch—ever a sin against life. The powerful effect of the poem derives from the oscillation between the confrontational address to Suffering and the idyllic description of the happy outside world as seen by the innocent girl she once had been not so very long ago.

Sabine's ghastly enemy has transformed this innocent blond girl into a pale ghost barely surviving her illness. When the pain becomes unbearable, Sabine utters a long, agonizing scream that connects her to all the world's suffering. In "Ah! Let Me Scream!" her vocabulary piles dissonance upon dissonance through a long and grating enumeration. The poet identifies with the slaughtered beast, with "the red hot iron when blacksmith hammers it," with "the harried tree / Ripped by the saw's teeth."[27] At the same time, she understands that she has become completely alone, forever cut off from the happy, healthy world she used to know. Like Jesus in the Olive wood, she faces her terrifying solitude, exhausted and sinking into despair. She tells her doctors: "I've suffered all I can, I can't go on. / Nothing left to believe, to hope for..."[28] In such despondent moments, compared to the sinister night surrounding her, death seems to offer salvation.

Yet Sabine loves life too much to linger very long on her despair. In her poetry, hope may vacillate to hopelessness, but it does not vanish. In "To Speak, to Tell You?" Sabine wishes to imitate the behavior of animals and plants, seeking comfort in silence away from unwelcome visitors. "I'd rather bear my suffering like a bird," she writes. Like the bird and the plant, she quietly waits though she does not know for what. The poem, pared down to an extreme simplicity, draws the reader into the same hushed waiting. Yet the last line dares utter the hope still living in Sabine: "The sun promised them to return, perhaps..."

The sun did return in the spring. Unexpectedly, as nature exploded in ritual revival, Sabine enjoyed a remission from her illness. In "Spring," her inner miracle answers that of nature with such force that she almost believes she has been cured. When a fearful voice resurfaces, reminding her of yesterday's agony, she silences it. Yesterday no longer exists; she turns toward tomorrow. "Once I've been cured," she cheerfully writes, "I'll want to see nothing but pretty things..."[29] She is again the lighthearted girl who believes in fairy tales, and delights in her own inventions. As she dreams of going to the Rose Festival at Nice, she creates a world of palaces, princes, and Rolls-Royces; with much wit she asks for a red swimming pool and cubist cushions. "I yearn for a life where fantasy's the rule," she declares.

But Sabine never went to Nice. She died on 12 July 1928, only a few months after the brief remission. Following her death, the Sicauds gathered the notebooks she had left behind. In the last one, they found very short untitled poems, fragments loosely written in free verses and built around images grounded in everyday life. Several are addressed to Vassili, the romantic companion Sabine imagined because she knew she would never grow old enough to meet him. Vassili is a Russian name, like Katia, Masha or Tania, Sabine's names in other lives. Being imaginary, Vassili can endure what Sabine's distraught mother cannot, and thus fulfill two roles: romantic creation and double. Each time Sabine addresses Vassili, she invokes life's simple joys as though forcing herself to remain attentive to "what the sun is singing." "Because you are cold tonight," she tells Vassili, "don't say there is no sun." It shines among the familiar objects that inspire Sabine's zest for life: a bit of straw, a cricket, an oil lamp, a church garden, or a pot of basil. Until the end, she finds comfort in these humble friends, imparting the force of a last will and testament into her otherwise fragmented poems. This is most visible in a rustic dialogue, which could recount an exchange between the poet and her mother, although the speakers remain anonymous. The brief answers echo the questions almost verbatim, thus creating a soothing, chanting effect; simultaneously, the use of the future tense evokes the inevitability of what is yet to come.

Sabine rarely mentions death directly. Instead, she speaks of absence, her mother's and her own. Each morning, staring at her bedroom door, she anxiously waits for her mother to enter and grant her another day. Her poem seems to bow under the weight of the unspeakable, its questions suspended, what is left out replaced by a pathetic plea: "Hold me tighter." The adolescent knows that soon her mother will stare at an empty chair, symbol of the absence of a girl torn away from a home where she completely belonged.

It is tempting to compare Sabine Sicaud to the better known adolescent Arthur Rimbaud, and yet the comparison may not be entirely appropriate considering that Sabine did not live to be seventeen, the age when Rimbaud started to write his revolutionary poetry. Still, one likes to think that the later Rimbaud—the vagabond gunrunner who died in dramatic and painful circumstances—would have recognized in Sabine one of the women poets whose coming he had announced in his letter to Paul Demeny, and that he would have welcomed "the strange, unfathomable, repulsive, delicious things" she had found to express her suffering.[30] Ironically, Sabine, like him, might later have abandoned poetry for something else—for cinema, perhaps... Who can say?

Many years have passed since Sabine departed. Alive, she was feted, published, and admired as a phenomenon. After her death in 1928, she became the victim of neglect and indifference. Neither Anna de Noailles nor Marcel Prévost, both of whom praised her so highly when she was alive, thought of collecting the poems Sabine wrote during her illness, and publishing them. The task was left to the Sicauds who, devastated by their sorrow, found refuge in a Buddhist commune in Nice. They returned to *La Solitude* in 1936, three years before the beginning of WWII. After the war and the death of her husband, Marguerite Ginet-Sicaud proceeded to gather and edit her daughter's unpublished poems with the help of professor and writer François Millepierres.[31] Their work was finally rewarded with the publication of Sabine's poems in 1958, thirty years after the poet's death.[32] Coincidentally, two years earlier, the poetry of child-poet Minou Drouet had been revealed to a public that proved to be more vicious than appreciative. Although the authenticity of Minou's poems had been established more than once, most famously through a public test given by France's Society of Authors, Composers and Music Publishers, many people preferred the idea of a literary hoax to the puzzling and vaguely threatening recognition of a child's unusual gifts. Adored by a few, brutalized by many, Minou eventually abandoned writing and celebrity for the safety of anonymity.[33] One cannot help wondering whether the same fate would have been reserved to Sabine if she had lived. Death may have spared her this humiliation. But with all eyes focused upon living child-poet Minou Drouet, Sabine's collection did not receive the attention it deserved, though it did stir the admiration of various writers, who included some of the poems in their anthologies, and thus insured their creator would not be forgotten.[34]

Sabine Sicaud may be the youngest poet ever to have written about extreme physical pain and imminent death. She bears witness to an experience that triggers primal emotions inside us all. Almost all the poems written during her illness rely on the immediacy of direct address that draw the reader to a world from which there is no escape. They come "at us" directly, painfully raw, without any abstraction that could lessen their emotional impact. The poet does not seek consolation in the possibility of another world. In the end, she finds relief where she had always found it: in her beloved home. Whether Sabine brings to life the wonders of *La Solitude* or rebels against her fate, her poetry remains as fresh today as when it was first written. It takes the reader through a wealth of emotions as it springs from the unique merging of a child's spontaneous vision of the world with the emotional and intellectual maturity of a truly accomplished poet.

NOTES

1. Robert Sabatier, *La Poésie du vingtième siècle*. Vol. 2. Paris: Albin Michel, 1982, pp. 160–61.

2. Sabine Sicaud, "Demain."

3. ——, "La Solitude."

4. ——, "La Solitude."

5. Marguerite Ginet-Sicaud, letter to Jacques Raphaël-Leygues, c. 1954.

6. *Ibid.* Unfortunately, the name of the tutor is not known.

7. Sabine Sicaud, "Premières feuilles."

8. ——, "La Solitude", translated by Norman R. Shapiro, as are all the translations of Sabine Sicaud's poems cited in this essay.

9. Louis Vaunois and Jacques Bour, *Les Poètes de la vie*. Paris; Corréa, 1945, pp. 36–37.

10. François Millepierres, *Introduction to Poèmes de Sabine Sicaud*. Paris: Stock, 1958, p. 12.

11. Rose Celli, "Sabine Sicaud", *Cahiers du Sud,* July 1939, pp. 553–556.

12. Suzanne took care of Sabine's mother at the end of her life and received the legal right to remain in *La Solitude.* Madame Ginet-Sicaud's will was registered in Villeneuve on 4 December 1959. It requested that all the letters and documents left behind be destroyed to protect the privacy of those yet living. When the heirs finally moved in, they burned or threw into the Lot river all the papers found after Madame Ginet-Sicaud's death, but they assured me the basket and its content were not among them. We can only conjecture as to what happened to the notebooks.

13. Pierre Adam, "Dix minutes avec une petite fille qui écrit des chefs-d'œuvre," *La Petite Gironde,* 8 July 1925. Maurice Rollinat, now almost forgotten but much admired in his life-time, published his most famous verses, *Les Névroses,* in 1883—twelve years after Rimbaud's *Le Bateau ivre.* Sabine may have enjoyed the unsettling portraits Rollinat made of animals like toads, cats, or owls. Indeed, she seems to emulate him to a certain extent in "Fafou." Verhaeren, national poet of Belgium at the time of his death in 1916, was very popular in France and, unlike Rollinat, is still appreciated to some extent today. In "Spring," Sabine borrowed directly Verhaeren's famous image of a boatman rowing toward his death (see note for "Spring").

14. "Lettre à Maurice Luxembourg," *Revue de l'Agenais* (1968): 69. Marguerite Fechner, nicknamed 'Daisy' by Madame Ginet-Sicaud, met Claude after Sabine's death and became his girlfriend. She eventually married someone else and had two sons (Jean and Christian Fechner), both film producers.

15. *Ibid.,* pp. 65–72.

16. Marguerite Dufaur, "Sabine Sicaud enfant et poète de génie," *La Dépêche,* 3 Apr.–26 May 1953, 1953.

17. "Demain."

18. *Revue du Jasmin d'Argent* (1924): 36.

19. *Poèmes d'enfant,* preface. Poitiers: Cahiers de France, 1926, p. 6.

20. Pierre Adam, *La Petite Gironde,* 8 July 1925.

21. *Mon Ciné* 209, 18 February 1926.

22. François Millepierres, "Commentaires," *Combat-Lettres,* 13 November 1958.

23. Ill-informed people have sometimes inacurately claimed that Sabine died of gangrene. Again, one must insist upon the fact that Sabine's foot did not display the type of lesion easily recognizable as gangrene. Her illness and the pain associated with it affected the bones.

24. Letter to Jacques Raphaël-Leygues.

25. Marcel Prévost, p. 37.

26. Marguerite Fechner, p. 70.

27. "Ah! Let Me Scream!"

28. "For the Doctors Who Come to See Me."

29. "Once I've Been Cured."

30. 13 May 1871, in *Rimbaud: Poésies complètes*. Paris: Livre de poche, 1998, p. 154.

31. Writer Rose Celli had first accepted to edit the poems, but personal problems forced her to abandon the idea. Another person, Georgette Converset, played an important part, considering that she copied by hand all the poems written by Sabine in order to provide a duplicate. Madame Ginet-Sicaud then typed all the poems for the publisher. During this editing process, it seems likely that minor changes were made to the final version of a handful of poems.

32. Marguerite Ginet-Sicaud was the last survivor of the Sicaud family. Gaston Sicaud died in 1942 and Claude Sicaud in 1949. Marguerite Ginet-Sicaud joined them in 1959, one year after the publication of Sabine's poems.

33. A recent article ("A Lost Child"), published by Robert Gottlieb in *The New Yorker* (November 6, 2006), pp. 70–77, recounts Minou's heartbreaking story.

34. All the anthologies listed in the bibliography contain a selection of Sabine's poems.

FIRST POEMS

Le Petit Cèpe

Va, je te reconnais, jeune cèpe des bois...
Au bord du chemin creux, c'est bien toi que je vois
Ouvrant timidement ton parapluie.
A-t-il plu cette nuit sur la ronce et la thuie?
Déjà, le soleil tendre essuie
Les plus hautes feuilles du bois...

Tu voulais garantir les coccinelles?
Il fait beau. Tu seras, jeune cèpe, une ombrelle,
L'ombrelle en satin brun d'un roi de Lilliput!
Ne te montre pas trop, surtout... Le chemin bouge... chut!
Fais vite signe aux coccinelles!

Des gens sont là, dont les grands pieds viennent vers toi.
On te cherche, mon petit cèpe...
Que l'ajonc bourdonnant de guêpes,
Le genièvre et le houx cachent les larges toits
De tes aînés, les frères cèpes,
Car l'un mène vers l'autre et la poêle est au bout!

Voici qu'imprudemment tout un village pousse:
Rouget couleur de sang, verdet couleur de mousse,
Girolle en bonnet roux,
Chapeaux rouges, verts, blonds, partout,
Les toits d'un rond village poussent!

Depuis l'oronge en oeuf, le frais pâturon blanc
Doublé de crépon rose,
Jusqu'au méchant bolet qu'on appelle Satan,
Je les reconnais tous, les joyeux, les moroses,
Les perfides, les bons, les gris, les noirs, les roses,
Tes cousins de l'humide automne et du printemps...

The Little Mushroom

Really now, little mushroom of the wood...
Beside the lane, I know it's you I see
Opening your umbrella timidly.
Did rain, last night, soak briar and greenery?
See how the gentle sun has stood
Drying the top leaves of the wood...

Sunshine... Now would you shield the ladybug?
Under your satin parasol—safe, snug—
She reigns like some fine king of Lilliput.
Don't show yourself... Shhh!... Something is afoot!
Danger! Quick, warn the ladybug!

Big-footed folk come, hunt you, probing-eyed.
If only you could tell the thistle,
Teeming with wasps, to buzz and bristle...
If juniper and boxwood could but hide
Those wide roofs of your elder mushroom brothers...
For, each one spied leads to the others,
And to the frying-pan they'll all be going!

A whole unwary village, sprouting, growing!
Blood-hued, moss-hued, chanterelles bonneted
In reddish brown... And every head,
In cap of red, of green, of yellow showing...
Rooftops of a round village growing!

The egg-shaped agaric, the pastern white,
Seersucker pink, no less.
Even the naughty devil's claw... Ah yes,
I know them all—those that distress, delight,
Or brood. Good, black, gray, pink... All of them, quite!
Kin spawned by spring's and fall's damp sultriness...

Mais c'est pour toi, cher petit cèpe, que je tremble!
Tu n'es encore qu'un gros clou bien enfoncé;
Ta tête a le luisant du marron d'Inde et lui ressemble.
Surtout, ne hausse pas au revers du fossé
Ta calotte de moine! on te verrait... je tremble.

Moi, tu le sais, je fermerai les yeux.
Exprès, je t'oublierai sous une feuille sèche.
Je t'oublierai, petit Poucet. Je ne puis, ni ne veux
Etre pour toi l'Ogre qui rêve de chair fraîche...
Je passerai, fermant les yeux!

Dans mon panier, j'emporterai quelques fleurs, une fraise...
Rien, peut-être... Mais toi, sur le talus,
A l'heure où les chemins se taisent,
Levant ton capuchon, tu ne nous craindras plus!

Brun et doré, sur le talus,
Tu t'épanouiras en coupole si ronde,
Si large, que la lune en marche—une seconde—
S'arrêtera pour te frôler de son doigt blanc. La nuit
Se fera douce autour de toi, bleue et profonde.
Migonne hutte de sauvage—table ronde
Pour les rainettes dont l'œil jaune et songeur luit,
Mon cèpe! tu ne seras plus un clou dans l'herbe verte,
Mais un pin-parasol dans l'ombre où se concertent
Les fourmis qui, toujours, s'en vont en longs circuits;
Tu seras une belle tente, grande ouverte,
Où les grillons viendront chanter, la nuit...

I fear for you, dear mushroom friend. I tremble!
Only a slim spike in the ground. Your crown
Glimmers with chestnuts' luster. Hide, dissemble!
Keep your monk's skullcap out of sight! Stay down!
Or else they're sure to see you... Oh, I tremble...

As for me, I'll just shut my eyes!
Leave you beneath your dry leaf, young Tom Thumb.
No ogre, I, with loud "Fee-fi-fo-fum",
Scheming for your fair flesh! No wise!
No! I'll pass by, keep mum, and shut my eyes...

I'll pick a flower or two, a berry, or
Nothing at all. And you will stand
Raising your cloak as silence falls, no more
To quake with fear before man's treacherous hand!

My little friend, there will you stand
Beside the path, all golden-browned,
Spreading out like a cupola, so round,
So wide, that, for a passing moment, soon
A white caressing finger of the moon
Will softly stroke you. And night's blue will lie
Strewn gently round you... Like some jungle hut
You'll stand beneath the deep and darkening sky;
Or, table for the tree toads all a-strut,
To light upon, cocking a yellow eye
A-gleam with dreaming... Little mushroom mine,
No more a slim spike in the green grass, but
Now, in the shade, a fair parasol-pine,
Where the ants come and go the whole night long;
Or a tent, open wide, of fine design,
Where crickets come to chirp their nighttime song...

Fafou

Chimère, dromadaire, kangourou?
Non. Rien que cette ombre chinoise,
Fafou, sur la fenêtre, à contre-jour, Fafou,
Toute seule et pensive... Un fuchsia pavoise
L'écran vert derrière elle, et j'entends, à deux pas,
Des oiseaux qui l'ont vue et s'égosillent.

Fafou se pose en gargouille. Un oeil las
Semble à peine s'ouvrir dans son profil où brille,
Cependant, quelque chose, on ne sait quoi d'aigu...
Par là, se cache un nid d'oisillons nus
Pour qui la mère tremble—Fafou songe.

Un tout petit pétale rouge, qui s'allonge,
Marque d'un trait sa gueule fine... Un bâillement.
Puis un autre... Fafou dormait *innocemment*.
Fafou dormait, vous dis-je! Elle s'étire,
La queue en yatagan,
Puis en cierge; le dos bombé, puis creux. Le pire,
C'est qu'elle n'a pas l'air de voir, s'égosillant,
La mère-oiseau dans l'if si proche...

Une patte en fusil, assise, la voilà
Qui se brosse, candide, et sa robe a l'éclat
D'un beau satin de vieille dame où se raccroche
La lumière du soir.
Une dame? ou quelque vieux diable en habit noir?

Fafou

Chimera, kangaroo, or dromedary?
No, just a shadow puppet, lolling
Against the light, pensive and stationary—
Fafou, alone, before the window, sprawling...
Beyond, the fuchsia-spangled greenery,
And birds, close by, that spy her, screeching, calling...

A gargoyle, there she squats. Heavy-eyed, she
Hardly raises a lid, head turned aside.
Still, something pierces through her glance, astride
The sill... The nest of hatchlings timidly
Hide as their mother trembles... Fafou muses.

A petal-tongue, pink, reaching out, is drawn
Over a fine-shaped snout. As Fafou snoozes—
Innocently, no doubt—she gives a yawn,
Then two... *Innocent? She?*... From tip to toe
Outstretched... Yatagan-like,
Her tail, now curved, now pointed, like a spike.
Her back, now arched, now slinging low.
What's more, she'll quite ignore that mother who
Screeches atop the nearby yew...

Paw shouldered, rifle-wise, there will she sit,
Simply brushing herself. Her black gown might
Be some old lady's, satin-sheened, as it
Catches the day's last rays of light.
Old lady's? Or some dandy's evening dress?

Fafou, je n'aime pas ces yeux d'un autre monde,
Ces yeux de revenant... Tout à l'heure croissants,
Maintenant lunes rondes,
Pourquoi ces trous phosphorescents
Dans cette face obscure ? Sur la toile
Qui se fonce, elle aussi—la toile du jardin
Où les pendants des fuchsias sont des étoiles—
La robe d'un noir vif s'éteint...

Elle n'est plus qu'un badigeon d'encre ou de suie,
Un pelage sinistre! Où l'as-tu pris
Ce noir d'enseigne de chat noir lavé de pluie?

Chat noir ou lion noir? Chauve-souris,
Chouette, quoi? Je ne sais plus. Sur la fenêtre,
Une tête où l'oreille plate disparaît...
Lézard, couleuvre ou tortue? Ah! si près,
L'oiseau même ne sait qui redouter, quel être
Fantastique et changeant va ramper cette nuit
Dans le jardin au noir mystère de caverne!

Du noir, du noir... Un point qui luit,
Deux points... deux vers luisants, vertes lanternes...
Fafou, je ne veux pas!
D'où reviens-tu, démon, de quel sabbat,
De quelle grotte de sorcière,
Lorsque tes yeux me font cette peur, tout à coup?

C'est l'heure des gouttières,
De la jungle! Foulant, d'un piétinement doux,
Une vendange imaginaire, sur la pierre,
Quelle arme aiguises-tu? Je ne veux pas, Fafou!
Viens sous la lampe! Un ruban rose au cou,
Un beau ruban de jeune fille, rose pâle,
Je te veux, comme en haut d'une carte postale,
Une petite chatte noire, voilà tout...

Fafou, those other-worldly eyes distress,
Disturb me... Ghostly eyes whose little crescents
Grow now to moons' full-roundedness.
Why those two holes, whose phosphorescence
Glows bright in that jet face? And there,
Out in the garden, where the dark greens wear
Their fuchsia stars, hanging a-glimmer...
And the gown's shadow-shine, grown dimmer, dimmer...

Nothing is she now but a giant blot,
A splash of soot, some fur piece ill-begot.
(Wherefrom, that rain-washed "Black Cat" tavern sign?)

Black cat? Black lion? Screech owl? Bat?
Who can tell? On her head, now lying flat,
Unseen, her ears... Some creature serpentine?
A lizard? Or a tortoise?... Ah! So near,
Yet mother bird scarce knows what she must fear.
What beast bizarre, what mutant will she see
Slinking, creeping around the garden ground
Tonight, steeped black in grotto mystery?

Black, black... An orb... No, two!... Gleam lustrously,
Two lanterns green! Two glow worms!... Ah! Confound
It all! Enough, Fafou!
Demon! Where have you been? What sabbath round?
What witches' den, so dark that you
Suddenly make me shrink, with fearsome glower?

Fafou, now is the jungle hour,
The time for rooftop-gutter wandering!
What weapon are you whetting, sharpening
Against the stones with pussyfooting tread,
Stamping a vintage in your mind outspread?
Enough, Fafou! Enough! Come by the lamp,
Pink-ribboned, like a young miss posing for
A postcard scene. I want you, little scamp...
You, my black cat, and nothing more.

La Châtaigne

Peut-être un hérisson qui vient de naître?
Dans la mer, ce serait un oursin, pas bien gros...
Ici, la boule d'un chardon—peut-être—
Ou le pompon sournois d'une bardane
Ou d'un cactus? Mais non, dans le bois qui se fane,
Dans le bois sans piquants, moussu, discret et clos,
Cette chose a roulé subitement, d'en haut,
Comme un défi... parmi les feuilles qui se fanent.

Allez, j'ai bien compris. C'est la saison.
Les geais, à coups de bec, ont travaillé dans l'arbre.
Même les parcs où veillent, tout pensifs, les dieux de marbre,
Ont de ces chutes-là, sur leurs gazons.

Marron d'Inde là-bas, châtaigne ici. Châtaigne
Rude et sauvage, verte encore, détachée
Par force de la branche où les grands vents, déjà, l'atteignent
Le vent et les geais ricaneurs, et la nichée
Des écoliers armés de pierres et de gaules.

Comme il faut se défendre! Sur l'épaule
De la douce prairie en pente, l'on pouvait
Glisser un jour, à son heure, qui sait?
Et se blottir dans un coin tiède, pour l'hiver...
Ah! pourquoi tant d'épines, tant d'aiguilles,
Tant de poignards dressés, pauvre peloton vert?
Une fente... Voici qu'un peu de satin brille
Et le cœur neuf est là, dessous, et rien ne sert
D'être châtaigne obscure, âpre au goût, si menue!
Fendue, on est une châtaigne presque nue...

The Chestnut

Perhaps a hedgehog, newly born? Maybe...
Or, in the sea, an urchin, rather small...
But here, a clump of thistle? Possibly
A burdock's sneaky little sphere? A ball
Of cactus?... No! None of them! Not at all!
This object, in the forest's velvety,
Mossy expanse of leaves discreetly dying,
Fell from on high, rolled suddenly, then, lying
Still, seemed to twit the fading greenery.

I know, this is the season. Jays have pecked
And picked over the tree, just as they do
In parks, before those gods of marble, who
Witness such fallings, mutely circumspect.

Horse chestnut, there; here, nutmeat soft—the kind
We love to eat, still green and growing wild—
Loosed from the branch by lusty winds that find
Them where they cling, or jeering jays reviled,
Or pole, or sling of many a naughty child...

Oh, how they must defend their skin! One day,
Who knows? They might go gliding down the mild,
Gently-inclined slope, wend their grassy way
And find a warm spot for snug winter rest...
What good, those spiny thorns, poor ball of green,
All your swords drawn? For there, about your breast,
A cut, the merest slit... And, dimly seen,
A bit of glossy satin, covering
Your young heart... Really now, what good is it
To be a chestnut, bitter, that will sit
Hidden in darkness, frail, if such a thing
As a thin slit can lay you open so?

Et le coup de sabot sur la tête viendra,
Et le couteau pointu, l'eau bouillante, le pot
Qui sue avec de petits rires, des sanglots
Dans les tisons trop rouges; tout sera
Comme il est dit en l'ordinaire histoire des châtaignes.

Et vous ne voudriez pas, quand me renseigne
Dans la ville brumeuse, un cri rauque: "marrons tout
    chauds!"
Quand j'aperçois, joufflus, blêmes, sans peau,
Ou craquelés et durs avec des taches de panthère,
Les frères de ma sauvageonne, tous ses frères—
Vous ne le voudriez pas, que j'évoque, là-bas,
Un vieil arbre perdant ses feuilles rousses,
Et me souvienne du choc sourd, lourd comme un glas,
De pauvres fruits tués qui tombent sur la mousse?

La Graine de raisin oubliée

Adieu, paniers! Les vendanges sont faites!
Qu'attends-tu, graine que je sais, doux grain vivant
Qui s'obstine, grain tendre?... C'est le temps!
Comme des castagnettes,
Claquent les feuilles sèches dans le vent.

Sur les côteaux, la vigne a chanté jusqu'au bout
Sa chanson rouge. Et, par toutes les routes,
Les chars s'en sont allés, comme ivres. Toutes,
Toutes les grappes ont saigné toutes leurs gouttes.

Qu'attends-tu, graine défiant l'Automne roux?

A voix basse chante le moût,
A voix haute le vigneron,

Soon, too, the stamping foot, the rough *sabot*
Down on your head... And oh! The pointed knife
Deep in your flesh... The water, boiling hot...
The sobs, the chortling laughs, the sweating pot
Over the flaming coals... A chestnut's life!

And, later, when I hear a lusty cry:
"Hot chestnuts! Get your chestnuts here!" When I
Spy, in the city mist, all of your brothers—
O wild one mine!—bloated, out of their skin,
So pale... Or when, perhaps, I see those others,
Crackling and hard, your panther-mottled kin,
Would you prefer that I not think again
Of an old tree losing its leaves of red,
And the dull knell that seemed to murmur when
Poor fruits fell, dying, to their mossy bed?

The Grape Left Behind

Bushels adieu! But why are you still there,
Lone, tender grape? The harvest's done. Now no
More vines to pick, my dear! It's time to go!
The dry leaves crackle in the air
Like castanets, a-click, a-clack...
But you? Why do you stubbornly hang back?

On the slopes vines sang out their scarlet song
Right to the end. The carts, rolling along,
Waddling on path and road, seemed drunk. And all,
Yes, all the grapes have bled their bodies dry.

Would you, proud seed, defy the ruddy fall?

Muffled, the new wine's hush-a-by;
Ringing, the joyous vintner's call;

A voix lointaine et sans entrain, la grive...

"Où faut-il maintenant qu'on vive?
Où faut-il? dit la grive. O raisins blonds,
Ô raisins noirs, ô raisins bleus!"

"Clic, clac! chantent les feuilles sèches,
La campagne couleur de pêche,
De miel et de framboise est déjà morte un peu.

Elle sera morte demain pour de longs jours..."

Te voilà cependant jeune et vivante,
Seule au cœur de la treille en loques, dans l'attente
D'on ne sait quoi d'heureux, graine de frais velours!

Graine de saphir moite à reflet de rubis,
Graine mûrie après les autres, retenue
Par une vrille folle entre deux branches nues,
Qu'attends-tu? Vois, le vent déchire les habits
Du somptueux platane. Tu subis,
Tu subiras le vent, tu subiras la pluie,
Le gel... "Qu'importent l'heure enfuie,
L'heure à venir, dis-tu, je vis..."

Et tu veux vivre,
Vivre, même boule de givre,
Même chair molle, avec des rides coulissant
Ta petite figure de négresse?
(Car tu deviendras vieille et noire; je pressens
Déjà ces choses tristes: la vieillesse,
Le ratatinement, l'ennui...) survivre là,
Dehors, parmi l'hiver aux longues plaintes,
Même noyée en éponge, cela
Tu le veux donc?... soit. L'homme et l'oiseau t'oublièrent.

Distant, the thrush's song, dour, dispossessed...

"Where would they have me go? Whereto?
Where shall I lie? Where shall I rest
My head, O grapes of white, O grapes of blue?
What shall I do, O grapes of black?"

"And the dry leaves sing their 'click-clack';
The countryside—raspberry hue,
Honey and peach—has died a little... See?

Dead will it be tomorrow, utterly..."

Still, there you cling, alive and ever young,
You, ragged vine's last grape—fresh, velvety—
Waiting for what good fortune, soon new-sprung?

Grape sapphire-moist with glints of ruby-rose;
Grape ripened late, after the rest, and fixed
To a dry tendril twisting wild, betwixt
Two bare limbs... Look! The wind rips at the clothes
Of the lush plantain. And you wait...
Why? What do you expect? What fate
Is yours, or will be? You survive
The wind, rain, ice... Past? Future?... What?
Time yet to come? Time vanished?... "But
What does it matter? I'm alive..."

Oh? Would you live
Despite the cost? For time does not forgive.
Soft ball of frost, you will grow old;
Wrinkled, your little negress face... Flesh cold
And black, shriveled in winter's loneliness,
Only to hear its plaintive sighs... Ah yes,
Winter, that dries you to a currant, or
Can drown you like a sponge! Is that
The life you want, forgotten more and more,
Unpicked, unplucked?... So be it then! Cling pat...
Men, birds ignored you, let you be...

Mais ne songes-tu pas à tant de grains, tes frères,
Tes frères dont le sang rouge ou doré s'en va
Par les grands chemins de la terre,
Vers les ports, les villes en feu, les bourgs, là-bas,
Là-bas, en tonneaux lourds ou flacons rares?
Tes frères, que sais-tu de leur vie, au delà
De ton étroit verger?

Vins brûlants ou mousseux, vins musqués, vins légers,
Vins qui sentent la rose et la mûre, et se parent
Des noms chantants de vieux pays... dis-moi,
Que sais-tu d'eux?–"Rien. Leur destin les mène.
Je vis; je ne suis qu'une graine...
J'attends, où tu me vois,
De tomber toute seule et de germer peut-être.
Le sillon me fera comme un nid, sous le toit
Du vieux cep grelottant, un nid où peut renaître
Une tige sauvage et libre... Je veux être
Encore jeune vigne aux beaux jours qui viendront!"

A pleine voix chante le vigneron,
A voix lointaine et plaintive, la grive...

But have you not a thought for family,
All your grape brothers, kin whose blood—gold, red—
Travels the globe in casks, in flagons rare,
To ports, cities aglow, towns spread out there
Over roads vast, unlimited?
Brothers? What do you know of those who fare
Far, far beyond your vineyard and your vine's
Narrow confines?

Wines burning to the tongue, wines sparkling, light,
Wines musky, berry-sweet, scented of rose,
Whose names sing of old lands... Tell me, what might
You know—poor grape like you—of those?
"Nothing. Their fate leads where it will. For me,
I live my life alone. As you can see,
I'm waiting for the moment when
I fall, ready no doubt to sprout again.
Till then, here in the furrow-nest I lie
Beneath chill-limbed old growth, till, by and by,
Come fairer days, I rise, young, wild, and strong!"

Ringing, the joyous vintner's song,
Distant and sad, the thrush's call...

Le Cytise

Non, pas une glycine. Au lieu de grappes mauves,
Ce sont des grappes d'or...
On dirait des pendants d'oreilles de jadis, en bel or fauve...
Ou des pastilles d'ambre, ou les confetti d'or
Qui joncheraient, pour un grand mariage,
Le tout petit sentier... C'est le décor
Où des torches s'allument. Vois flamber le paysage!

Survient le vent.
Et c'est une cascade lumineuse de topazes,
Un long feu d'artifice, un jet d'eau qui s'embrase,
Un Quatorze Juillet de mai! Vois, dans le vent,
La joie ardente du printemps!

Pas de canons, d'ailleurs, ni de Bastilles prises.
C'est la fête rustique du Cytise.

En cheveux de soleil,
Papillotes, jeune perruque ébouriffée
Le Cytise s'éveille. Il est pareil
A quelque page blond sortant d'un magique sommeil.

Il fut un arbre mort et le voici pareil
Au Printemps même, secouant sa tête ébouriffée...
Lancés par la main d'un Génie, ou par les fées,
C'est l'éparpillement de petits sabots jaunes, si légers,
Si menus et vernis, qu'ils émerveillent
Le vieux cyprès bourru, chaussé de brun. Et les abeilles
Vont et viennent, avec ce bruit que l'on entend dans les
        vergers.
Et moi, comme toi, vieux cyprès, je m'éverveille
Longtemps, devant cela, que nul ne semble voir—
Sauf nous deux—le jeune cytise en fleurs, au bord du soir.

The Laburnum

No, not wisteria's clustered lavender.
Rather, clusters of gold...
Like antique earrings, yesteryear's, that were
Wrought of a lovely, deeply tawny gold...
Amber pastilles, golden confetti, spreading
Over the lane, as if for some grand wedding
Décor... Torches flaming the scene... Behold!

And then, the breeze.
A bright topaz-cascade, firework display,
Water-jets' glow, July fourteenth in May!
Behold! Light everywhere! And, in the breeze,
Springtime's hot-blooded revelries!

No guns, no captured Bastille edifice!
A wakening! Rustic fete, this!

Laburnum of the sunshine hair—
Tousled young wig, curlpapers twirling round—
Awakes, looks like some page lad, blond and fair,
Roused from a magic sleep. And, standing there,

Like a dead tree, but born anew, and fair
Once more, shaking its tousled head round, round,
Like Spring, reborn... And, strewn over the ground
By Genie's hands or fairies', see the tiny,
Light, golden slippers, lying bright, so shiny
That they astound that grumpy, gruff old coz—
The cypress, shod in brown. And soon, abuzz,
The bees abound, go flitting here, there, fly,
With that sound that an orchard always makes... And I
Stand awed, like you, old tree,
As no one, none but you and me—
Or so it seems—pays any mind to him,
Blooming laburnum at the evening's rim.

Le Tamaris

Tout l'hiver, le laurier t'a bravé. Tout l'hiver,
Les deux ifs, s'éventant de leurs franges épaisses,
Tout dit: "N'aimes-tu pas cette fraîcheur de l'air?"

Et le cèdre était vert, le cyprès était vert,
Et les bambous avaient des gestes d'allégresse,
Et le palmier jouait à l'oasis...

Et le lierre en habit vert bouteille, et la mousse
En laine vert grenouille, et l'herbe vert maïs,
Te narguaient, en couvrant le sol brun d'une housse,
Où le givre cousait des boutons de cristal...

Et le magnolia de faïence vernie,
Le fusain compassé, l'yucca de métal,
Regardaient avec ironie
Tes rameaux grelottants... Le buis même, le buis
Des bons vieux jardinets de presbytère,
Semblait fat et repu sur un morceau de terre
Large comme la main—et "l'artichaut des puits"
Encadrait le bassin de roses agressives...

Et tous disaient: "Voyez, grâce à nos feuilles vives,
Ce n'est jamais l'hiver, jamais l'hiver!"

Et devant toi, si découvert,
Si nu, si maigre, avec de petits doigts si frêles,
Je m'arrêtais, ne sachant plus...

The Tamarisk

The laurel, winter long, teased you, stood bold.
Wafting their thick-tressed fringe, so too the yews.
Everything said: "Don't you just love the cold?"

Cypress and cedar, green. And the bamboos,
Fanning gestures of joy, would turn and toss.
The palm feigned its oasis-play...

Dressed bottle-green, the ivy. And the moss,
Like frog-green wool... Corn-green, the grass. And they
Twitted you as the dark, cover-clad ground
Shone with frost-crystal buttons sewn all round...

And the magnolia's porcelain brilliancy,
The snug-crouched bush, the yucca tough as steel,
All looking at you sneeringly,
Jeering at you, at how cold you must feel,
With shivering twigs... Even the boxwood, showing
Off on the nice old parsonage's land—
On garden plots no wider than a hand—
Looked smug, well fed... Wild artichoke leaves, growing,
Hurling their rosebud berries round the pond...

And all cried out: "See? There's no winter season!
No wintertime! No, none! And we're the reason!"

I stopped. I could not move beyond
You, standing so defenseless there,
Your fingers, frail and small, your body, bare...

Mon arbrisseau léger, dont le front chevelu
Frisé par la brise de mer aux tièdes ailes,
Prenait là-bas, dans le soleil, un vert si doux,
Un vert qui se teintait de rose à tous les bouts
Dès que le temps des fleurs ouvrait sa boîte à poudre
Et son étui de rouge parfumé,
Faudrait-il se résoudre
A ne plus voir ton fin visage ranimé?

Ah! qu'ils m'importent peu, les autres, les tenaces,
Les toujours verts, si tu dois rester nu!
Comprendront-ils jamais ce qu'il y a de grâce,
De charme délicat dans tes bourgeons menus
Lorsque tu ressuscites,
Mon tamaris, pour qui l'hiver est bien l'hiver...
D'avoir tremblé pour toi, comme on se penche vite
Sur ce premier duvet imperceptible hier,
Et comme on t'aime pour ce vert, ce tendre vert
Si miraculeusement neuf, après l'hiver...

My little tree, so light of limb, whose brow—
Its locks curled by the warm-winged sea-breeze air—
Turned such a soft green in the sun, tinged now
An autumn rose... Once blossom-time saw fit
To spread its rouge and dab its powder-puff
Here, there, and everywhere, is it
Possible you had had enough,
That you will spring to life no more?

Who cares about the hardy ones? All those
Who, evergreen, never need doff their clothes?
Are they clever enough to know what store
Of grace, of tender charm, your buds possess
When they, risen again, profess:
"Ah! Thanks to me,
Winter is winter, and will ever be!..."
My tamarisk! We feared so much for you!
We gaze now at that velvet down, scarce seen,
And love you for that miracle of green,
After the winter's death, reborn anew...

Matin d'automne

C'est un matin... non pas un matin de Corot
Avec des arbres et des nymphes—sur la terre,
C'est un coin tout petit, entre des murs de pierres
Pas bien hauts...
C'est un matin dans le petit jardin du presbytère.

C'est un matin d'automne:
Vigne rouge, dahlias jaunes,
Petits doigts tortillés de chrysanthèmes roux;
Chute de pièces d'or sous l'aubépine, au bout;
Un tournesol montrant sa face de roi nègre
Sous un vieux diadème en plumes raides, un peu maigres...
Arrosoir vert, près du géranium en pot.
C'est un matin, sans nymphes de Corot.

Le curé dort, la maison dort, le chemin dort,
Pendant que, doucement, tombent des pièces d'or...

C'est un matin d'automne...
L'aube, qui s'est levée à pas de loup, d'abord frissonne
En peignoir rose... puis se met à rire dans le ciel,
Et tout devient rose comme elle, et rit comme elle,
Et ce sont des clartés roses et blondes telles
Que le petit jardin doré semble irréel.
Réveillée en sursaut, dans le clocher, la cloche sonne:
"Vite! vite! Levez-vous, bonnes gens!
C'est le matin! C'est le matin d'automne!
Je sonne! Il fait beau temps!

Entends, vieille servante en bonnet blanc, du presbytère,
C'est l'heure, lève-toi... Lève-toi, vieux curé;
Vois les oiseaux, vois la lumière!
Prends ta soutane et ton bonnet carré,
Ouvre ta porte et va... L'heure te presse!

Autumn Morning

One of those mornings... But not a Corot,
With nymphs out lolling on the green, and trees...
Only a corner of the rectory's
Garden—a little space between
Stone walls built low.

One of those autumn mornings... Scene
With yellow dahlias, reddish vines
Whose every little finger intertwines
With ruddy-hued chrysanthemum.
A shower of gold coins falling to the ground
Beneath the hawthorn... Sunflower meager-crowned,
Stiff-plumed tiara round the face of some
Black king!... And next to the geranium,
An old green watering-can. And so,
One of those mornings... Nymphless, not Corot.

Curé and house and road: everything joins
In sleep, as gently fall the golden coins...

One of those autumn mornings. Day
Creeps on her silent feet in négligée
Of pink... Trembles at first, then laughs. The sky
Grows pink too, laughs. And by and by
The blond and rosy splendor will reveal
The garden, all in gold, almost unreal.
Jolted awake, the bell chimes in the steeple,
Warning: "Get up! Get up, good people!
It's morning! A fine autumn morning, hear?

"You, in the rectory... Old Mademoiselle,
Ding dong! Ding dong! Get up, my dear!
Off with your nightcap! You, *mon père*, as well...
Look! See the birds, the sun? Quick! Quick! Put on
Your cassock, your biretta... Out!... Begone!
The hour draws near!

L'allée a tous les tons fauves des vieux missels...
Va vite, ne t'attarde pas, sous le grand ciel,
Au tout petit jardin plein d'allégresse...
Couleur de feu, couleur de fleurs, couleur de miel,
Il est trop beau! tu le prendrais pour un autel.
Tu manquerais la messe..."

Les Papillons de jour

Dans le ciel, une fleur de fève,
Qui tourne et vole et cabriole...
Flocons passant en farandoles
Que la brise soulève...

Ailes s'ouvrant comme des yeux...
Papillons blancs, papillons bleus,
Qu'attire l'odeur des corolles...
Fleurs qui volent et cabriolent!

Gais feux d'artifice lancés
Dans la campagne, sur les haies;
Saphirs et rubis des futaies
Par un coup de vent dispersés...

Dans le ciel, une fleur de fève.

"The path lies, tawny-hued,
Like missels, drab with age. Don't loll, *mon père,*
Beneath the sky decked in its festive mood,
All fire and flowers and honey! Ah! Too fair!
You'll think you see the altar there!... Alas!
Careful, or you could miss the mass!"

Daytime Butterflies

A beansprout's skyward vagaries,
Cutting its capers, twisting, twirling...
Flakes in a farandole, fly, whirling
Over the fluttering breeze...

And wings that open wide like eyes...
White butterflies, blue butterflies,
Drawn by corolla-scents unfurling.
Flowers a-flitting, twisting, twirling...

Gay fireworks shooting here and there
Over the rustic hedges, trees...
Shrub-borne sapphires and rubies, these,
Blown on a sudden gust of air...
A beansprout's skyward vagaries...

La Chèvre

L'herbe est si fraîche, ce matin,
Que son velours tendre nous hante—
Son velours neuf qui sent la menthe,
Le jeune fenouil et le thym.

La vache s'étire, gourmande,
Vers le champ de trèfle voisin.
Tous les verts bordent le chemin
Du vert acide au vert amande.

Mais c'est un velours trop soigné
Qui s'aligne entre les clôtures...
Dans les ronces, à l'aventure,
La chèvre aime s'égratigner.

Elle aime le vert des broussailles
Où l'ombre devient fauve un peu,
Et ce vert d'arbres presque bleus
Que tous les vents d'orage assaillent.

C'est bien au delà des sillons
Et des vergers gorgés de sèves,
Que les clochettes de son rêve
Eparpillent leurs carillons...

Parfois, un glas les accompagne...
Mais il fait beau, c'est le matin!
Chevrette de Monsieur Seguin
Ne regardez pas la montagne...

The Goat

Cool is the grass this morning; our
Sense yields to its smooth redolence,
Like velvet, tender mid the scents
Of mint, and thyme, and fennel flower.

The glutton cow yearns toward the clover.
Greens—acid-tart and almond green,
And all the shades that lie between—
Follow the path, border it over.

Too tender and too neat, alas,
To please the goat, penned in. For she
Would much prefer to saunter free
And scratch against the prickly grass.

She loves the brambles' green, unfenced,
Where shadows cast a tawny hue;
The green of trees, turned almost blue,
That storm winds howl and pound against.

Far from these furrows, wandering on;
Far from the sap-rich orchards these;
The dream-bells of her reveries
Sprinkle their tinkling carillon...

At times a knell too fills the air,
Though fair the morning... Ah! Daudet's
Little goat! Please, I pray you gaze
Not on the mountain-top out there...

La Bruyère

O bruyère, bruyère,
Je croyais te connaître et je ne savais rien
De cette odeur mêlée à la rumeur légère
Qui vient du fond des pignadas, qui vient
Des longs pays qui sont les tiens, bruyère...

Je connaissais ta petite âme de chez nous,
Ta petite âme éparse au pied de chênes roux
Et de sorbiers déjà couleur d'automne...

Mais ce rose éclatant, ces violets pourprés,
Ces épis de corail aux grains serrés,
Cette lumière en fins grelots qui sonnent,
Les trouve-t-on chez nous—même l'automne?

Ici, les pins tendent si haut leurs parasols
Que les vents de la dune se prélassent
Et que le soleil joue à pile ou face,
Librement, sur tes chauds tapis couvrant le sol...

Et c'est comme une flamme au ras des sables,
Un couchant rouge et mauve interminable
Sous les hauts parasols,
Quand tu fleuris, bruyère...

Tes fleurs... tes fleurs sont le tapis
D'un temple ouvert, bourdonnant de prières...
Entre les piliers bruns, des parfums assoupis
D'encens et de résine,
Des parfums d'immortelle et de mousse marine
Accompagnent le tien, bercé dans l'air...

Et ton âme d'ici, je la découvre
De ce wagon-joujou courant près de la mer,
Au seuil de ces pays roses et verts
Qui s'ouvrent
Sur le vert et le rose argentés de la mer...

Côte d'Argent, 1925

The Heather

O heather, heather mine!
I thought I knew you, but I really knew
Nothing about the fragrant scent that you
Combine with rustlings from your groves of pine
Deep in your bristling thickets, briar mine...

I knew that modest soul that you spread round
About our home-grown oaks and russet-browned
Ash trees that, early, boast the shades of fall...

But this bold pink, this violet, crimson-glowing—
Coral pods packed with seeds to overflowing—
And this rare light, tinkling like bells... Is all
This what we find at home, even in fall?

Here, pines raise parasols high overhead
As the dune winds blow, lazing languidly,
And the sun, throwing heads or tails, makes free
Over your carpets, warm and wide outspread...

And when you bud and blossom, heather, why,
The sands seem all aflame with sunset red
And mauve against the sky
Beneath each parasol...

Your flowers... Carpeting a temple hall
Open wide and a-buzz with prayers intense...
Brown pillars with incense and resin scents,
Languorous, wafting airily
A perfume blending your own gentle smell
With salty sea moss and sweet *immortelles*...

And it's your soul I find as I stroll free
In my toy wagon by the rolling sea,
Here, at the threshold of your pink, green sands
That stretch their hands
Out to the silvery greens, pinks of the sea...

Côte d'Argent 1925

Les Pélerins de la dune

Les pins... Les pins aux verts cheveux,
Aux sandales d'or et de cuivre,
Un par un, deux par deux,
Droit devant eux,
S'en vont, comme ivres...

Ivres de soleil, et de vent,
Les bras tendus, penchés souvent,
Tant le vent du large les pousse,
Tant le soleil mord jusqu'au sang
La dune rousse.
Les pins s'en vont, chargés d'encens,
D'or et de myrrhe, vers là-bas,
Vers des pays qu'on ne sait pas, tendant les bras...

Les pins s'en vont dans un bruit d'ailes,
Un bruit de pas, un bruit de voix surnaturelles.

Je les entends, je les entends... à pas légers,
La forêt suit, comme un troupeau suit le berger.
A voix basse, bouche fermée,
Comme les chanteurs de l'Ukraine,
L'Océan dit ses peines.

La dernière houle, calmée
Froisse et défroisse des étoffes qu'elle traîne...
Et le vent joue à l'imiter, dans les remous
Des pins en marche.

O patriarches,
Verts pèlerins des sables roux,
Pèlerins vers je ne sais où,
C'est bien vous qui marchez, c'est vous
Qui faites, sous mes orteils nus, frémir la dune...

The Pilgrims of the Dune

The pines, with their straightforward air—
Amber their sandals, green their hair—
Amble their way
In single file or pair by pair,
Drunk, some might say...

Drunk with the sun, drunk with the breeze,
Their arms outstretched before them, these
Pilgrims will bow, at times, wind-smitten.
And by the burning sun hard-bitten,
The sun that gnaws
The rust-hued dunes with bloody jaws...
Off they go, bearing incense, gold, and myrrh,
Toward far-off, unknown lands, these *voyageurs*...

Off they go in a muffled sound, like wings,
And steps, and other-worldly mutterings...

I hear them, light of tread... The wood proceeds
To follow, sheep-like, as the shepherd leads.
Tight-lipped, the Ocean drones its pain
Like those *bassi profundi* from Ukraine.
Calmed now, the final swell.

Wrinkles and smooths the sailcloth in its wake...
The winds, like pine trees marching forth pell-mell
   shudder and shake.

O worthies of the ages!
You pilgrims of the ruddy dunes! Green sages
En route to what far-distant lands?
O patriarchs! It's you who make
My bare feet quiver with the shivering sands...

Le soir tombe... Et peut-être ici
A-t-on rêvé, mouillés de lune,
De soirs mauves, gris pâle aussi,
Et diaphanes...
De vos soirs, Puvis de Chavannes...

Moi, j'ai vu des pins, un par un,
Devenir bleus, devenir bruns,
Je les ai vus, fouettés d'embruns,
Disloqués par le vent sauvage,

Et conduisant toujours, toujours,
Le même long pèlerinage...

Hallucinés, aveugles, sourds,
Je les ai vus en Don Quichotte,
Je les ai vus en Juif-errant,
Chauves, bossus, manchots, branlants,
Ombres chinoises de la côte...

Et derrière, j'ai vu, pressés
Comme les moutons de la fable,
D'autres pins, tous les pins blessés,
Cramponnés aux pentes de sable...

Dans les pots d'argile, saignait
Leur sève épaisse, goutte à goutte...
Les premiers pins suivaient leur route.

Moi seule les accompagnais...
Vers quelle Espagne de miracles?
Vers quelles sierras, quels châteaux,
Quels tabernacles?

Evening falls... This could be where we
Have dreamed a moon-bathed reverie
Of evenings mauve, pale gray, like those,
Diaphanous,
That Puvis de Chavannes has given us...

I've watched as each pine slowly goes
To blue, then brown. Each gale that rose,
Howling, over the waves, would spread
Its spray about them, buffeted.

Persistent, on and on they plied
The long, unceasing pilgrimage...

I saw each pine-tree personage—
Some deaf, some blind, or nightmare-eyed
Wandering Jew, Quixotic Don,
Humpbacked, bald, halt, one-armed—press on,
Coastward, in puppet silhouette—

And in the rear I saw—thick set
And clinging to the hillside sand,
Like sheep that dwell in Fable Land—
The last ones, wounded to the quick...

Into clay pots they bled their thick
Sap, dripping droplets, one by one...
The first marched on in unison.

And I alone went with them. Where?
What Spanish miracles lay there?
What bold sierras, fine *châteaux*,
What holy shrines?

Non, ne me dites pas tout haut
L'histoire des pins sur la dune,
L'histoire vraie en quatre mots...

Puisque je vois, au clair de lune,
Au clair du soleil, verte ou brune,
Marcher la forêt devant moi...
Puisque c'est vrai, lorsque j'y crois...

Côte d'Argent, août 1925

La Chanson du petit caillou

On le croit silencieux; moi je sais qu'il chante.
Il chante, au bord du chemin, sa chanson de petit caillou.
Mais comme il chante a voix basse, les hommes, d'ordinaire,
n'en savent rien.
A-t-il appris dans la rivière, ou sur le barrage du ruisseau,
les secrets de l'eau qui court? A-t-il appris le long de la
route, les secrets des êtres qui passent?

No need to tell me where they go,
These pilgrims of the dune, these pines...
I know, I know it must be so...

Moonlit or sunlit, brown or green,
They march before my eyes. The scene
Leaves little doubt! For, lo! I see it...
If I believe it... Then so be it!

Côte d'Argent, August 1925

The Little Pebble's Song

They think he's silent. Me, I know he's singing,
Singing beside the path his little pebble song.
But since he sings so softly, people really
have no idea...
Did he learn in the stream, or on the brooklet's dam,
the flowing waters' secrets? Or did he learn, along
the road, the secrets of creatures passing by?

Le Funiculaire de la Rhune

Joujou de bois verni, le petit train se hisse
Par des chemins à lui, dont on s'effraye un peu,
Vers le sommet qui semble fuir, lilas et bleu...
L'air vif sent l'arnica, le baume et la réglisse.
Joujou de bois verni, le petit train se hisse.

Les moutons étonnés le regardent venir...
On les dirait pourtant—lui de bois, eux, de laine—
Pris au même bazar, dans les boîtes d'étrennes.
Un rayon de soleil s'amuse à revernir
Chaque fois, le joujou qu'ils regardent venir.

Dans le bas, s'assombrit la gorge romantique
Où dort, tapi, le toit de bruns contrebandiers.
Au loin, des pics ont l'air en neige d'amandiers;
Et, sur toute la côte où danse l'Atlantique,
C'est le galop de grands nuages romantiques.

Pays Basque et sierras... l'Amérique, au delà
De ce voile d'argent, pointillé de navires.
Chenille à cinq anneaux, le train-joujou s'étire
Vers la cime où le bleu s'estompe de lilas...
Vois-tu cette eau d'argent—l'Amérique au delà—

Vois-tu ce vert des prés, ce jaune de la dune,
Ce brun des pignadas, ces blancheurs de villas,
Saint-Jean-de-Luz, Biarritz et Bayonne, et cela
Qui règne ici déjà, par moitié, sur la Rhune,
Cette couleur d'Espagne où se chauffe la dune?...

The La Rhune Funicular

Shiny wood toy, steep climbs the train up there,
Crawling along its way, uneasily,
Toward the peak, lilac-blue, that seems to flee...
Arnica, licorice, balm fill the crisp air.
Shiny wood toy, steep climbs the train up there.

The sheep, agape, watch it creeping its way,
Though both could be—one wood, the others wool—
Bought from the same bazaar, toyshop chock full.
The sun darts now and then a playful ray,
Shining the toy they watch creeping its way.

Below, in shadowed gorge, in stance romantic,
The swarthy smugglers' hut sleeps, shroud-enwrapped.
Far off, summits like almond-trees, snowcapped...
And, on the coast where prances the Atlantic,
Great clouds go galloping their dance romantic.

Sierras, Pays Basque... America, due west,
Behind that silvered veil dotted with ketches.
Five-ringed, the toy-train caterpillar stretches
Summitward, to the lilac-blurred blue crest...
Silver waves... Look! America, due west...

See? Meadows green, the yellow of the dune,
Pignadas brown, white villas strewn, Bayonne,
Saint-Jean-de-Luz, Biarritz... And there, upon
Half of the land, reigning over La Rhune,
That Spanish hue, glowing, warming the dune?

Entre deux rocs géants, Don Quichotte apparaît.
Sens-tu, sens-tu le vent qui vous glace et vous brûle—
Qui vous brûle à midi, vous glace au crépuscule—
Acharné sur ta cape, arrachant nos bérets?...
Sur l'aile des moulins, Don Quichotte apparaît.

La clochette du train sonne comme une folle...
C'est l'heure... Descendons. Le petit train s'en va.
Là-haut, resté debout, moderne Quebranta,
Mi sur terre française et mi sur l'espagnole,
Le marchand de biscuits—"Adios, señorita!"—
Regarde gravement le joujou qui s'en va
Avec son *esquila* tintant comme une folle.

Between two boulders Don Quijote stands.
And that wind... Do you feel it burning, freezing—
Burning at noon, freezing at dusk—and seizing
Shawls and berets, tugging with wrenching hands?...
See? Windmill wings... There Don Quijote stands.

Time to return. The train's clanging her bell,
Pêle-mêle... Come, down we go. The little train's
Leaving... The pastry-man, one foot on Spain's
And one on France's soil—"Adios, mam'zelle!"—
Astride, Quebranta-like, staunchly remains
Atop the peak, watching the plaything-train's
Descent, a-crawl, as wildly clangs her bell.

LA SOLITUDE

La Solitude

Solitude... Pour vous cela veut dire seul,
Pour moi—qui saura me comprendre?
Cela veut dire: vert, vert dru, vivace tendre,
Vert platane, vert calycanthe, vert tilleul.

Mot vert. Silence vert. Mains vertes
De grands arbres penchés, d'arbustes fous;
Doigts mêlés de rosiers, de lauriers, de bambous,
Pieds de cèdres âgés où se concertent
Les bêtes à Bon Dieu; rondes alertes
De libellules sur l'eau verte...

Dans l'eau, reflets de marronniers,
D'ifs bruns, de vimes blonds, de longues menthes
Et de jeune cresson; flaques dormantes
Et courants vifs où rament les "meuniers";
Rainettes à ressort et carpes vénérables;
Martin-pêcheur... En mars, étoiles de pruniers,
De poiriers, de pommiers; grappes d'érables.
En mai, la fête des ciguës,
Celle des boutons d'or: splendeur des prés.
Clochers blancs des yuccas, lances aiguës
Et tiges douces, chèvrefeuille aux brins serrés,
Vigne-vierge aux bras lourds chargés de palmes,
Et toujours, et partout, fraîche, luisante, calme,
L'invasion du lierre à petits flots lustrés
Gagnant le mur des cours, les carreaux des fenêtres,
Les toits des pavillons vainement retondus...
Lierre nouant au front du chêne, au cou du hêtre,
Ses bouquets de grains noirs comme un piège tendu
A la grive hésitante; vert royaume

La Solitude

"Solitude"... It's a word that, for you, means
One thing. But for me, can you understand?
It means green! Green! Deep greens, greens bright or bland,
Plane-tree greens, calycanthus, linden greens...

Green word, green silence, green the hands of trees,
Tall, leaning... Bushes' finger curlicues—
Rosebushes, laurels, and bamboos—
Entwined... Old cedars' feet, where devotees—
Ladybugs!—congregate, betwixt, between,
Where dragonflies flit, skim the waters green...

And, in the water, chestnut trees reflected,
Blond wicker, long-stemmed mint, brown yews,
Young cress; water in sleeping pools collected,
Or currents briskly flowing; chub-fish whose
Fins row like oars; toads leaping, springing;
Carp full of years, kingfishers too... Look! See
How lovingly each month of March keeps bringing
To life the star-leafed plum, pear, apple-tree,
Clusters of maples... And, in May,
Gold-budded hemlocks in festive display
Of meadow splendor! Yuccas rising high,
White steeples, lances sharp against the sky
On slender shafts... And honeysuckle's tight
Mass of small sprigs, and creeping virgin vine,
Arms heavy with its leaves... Everywhere, bright
And fresh, and peaceful... Calm, the serpentine
Ivy invasion, wave on wave, that reaches,
In time, the courtyard walls, each widow-pane,
The very farmhouse roofs, clipped clean in vain...
Ivy binding the oak's brow and the beech's
Slim neck; dark berries spread out in bouquets
Like traps to seize and overwhelm
The hesitant and wary thrush; green realm

Des merles en habit—royaume qui s'étend
Ainsi que dans un parc de Florence ou de Rome
En nappes d'émeraude et cordages flottants...
Lierre de cette allée au porche de lumière
Dont les platanes séculaires, chaque été,
Font une longue cathédrale verte—lierre
De la grotte en rocaille où dorment abrités
Chaque hiver, les callas et les cactus fragiles;
Housse, que la poussière blanche de la ville
Givre à peine les soirs de très grand vent—pour moi,
Vert obligé des vieilles pierres,
Des arbres vieux des toits qui penchent, des vieux toits.

Un château? Non, Madame, une gentilhommière,
Un ermitage vert qui sent les bois, le foin,
Où les bruits de la route arrivent d'assez loin
Pour n'être plus qu'une musique en demi-teintes.
Un train sur le talus se hâte avec des plaintes,
Mais l'horizon tout rose et mauve qu'il rejoint
Transpose le voyage en couleurs de légende.
On regarde un instant vers ces trains qui s'en vont
Traînant leur barbe grise—et c'est vrai qu'ils répandent
Un peu de nostalgie au fil de l'été blond...

Mais le jazz des moineaux fait rage dans les feuilles,
Les pigeons blancs s'exaltent, le cyprès
Est la tour enchantée où des notes s'effeuillent
Autour du rossignol. Du pré
Monte la fièvre des grillons, des sauterelles,
Toutes les herbes ont des pattes, ont des ailes.
Et l'Ane et le Cheval de la Fable sont là
Et Chantecler se joue en grand gala
Jour et nuit dans la cour où des plumes voltigent.

Of blackbirds, formal-dressed, realm that arrays
Its wealth in gardens—Roman, Florentine—
In emerald layers, flowing vine to vine...
Ivy twined round a façade brightly lit
Along the tree-lined path, whose hundred-year
Plane trees will, every summer, make of it
A green cathedral; ivy from the drear
And craggy grotto, where the calla lily
And cactus frail doze safe in winter sleep;
Coverlet frosted with a white and frilly
Dusting of powder that night gusts will sweep
Out from the city... And, for me, that very,
Utterly green, that green most necessary,
Of old rocks, roofs sloping and old, old trees...

A *château*? No, madame. Just one of those
Lodges, green, with a scent, a hint
Of woods, of hay, where road cacophonies
Dim in a distant music's mezzotint...
A train goes whining by. Way off, the rose
And mauve horizon will blend and transpose
Its trail to colors legendary... There,
We glance a moment at each train that goes
Dragging its beard behind, graying the air,
Strewing nostalgia through blond summer's hair...

Among the leaves sparrows twitter their jazz,
Doves coo their joy, the cypress has
Become the enchanted tower, where notes go falling,
Leaf-like, before the nightingale...
Grasshoppers, crickets, chirp their fitful calling
Round and about the grassy vale,
Whose every blade has wee legs, tiny wings...
The fable's Ass and Horse are there. And, yes,
Chantecleer, night and day, in fancy dress,
Feathers the courtyard with his flutterings.

Au clair de l'eau, c'est l'éternel prodige
Du têtard de velours devenu crapaud d'or,
De la voix de cristal parmi les râpes neuves
D'innombrables grenouilles. Le chat dort,
Dickette-chien s'affaire, et sur leur tête pleuvent
Des pastilles de lune ou de soleil brûlant.
S'il pleut vraiment, la pluie à pleins seaux ruisselants
S'éparpille de même aux doigts verts qui l'arrêtent.

Un tilleul, des bambous. L'abri vert du poète.
Du vert, comprenez-vous? Pour qu'aux vieilles maisons
Rien ne blesse les yeux sous leurs paupières lasses.
Douceur de l'arbre, de la mousse, du gazon...
Vous dites: Solitude? Ah! dans l'heure qui passe,
Est-il rien de vivant plus vivant qu'un jardin,
De plus mystérieux, parfumé, dru, tenace,
Et peuplé–si peuplé qu'il arrive soudain
Qu'on y discourt avec mille petits génies
Sortis l'on ne sait d'où, comme chez Aladin.

Un mot vert... Qui dira la fraîcheur infinie
D'un mot couleur de sève et de source et de l'air
Qui baigne une maison depuis toujours la vôtre,
Un mot désert peut-être et desséché pour d'autres,
Mais pour soi, familier, si proche, tendre, vert
Comme un îlot, un cher îlot dans l'univers?

In the bright watershine, life's elemental,
Eternal miracle transforms the gentle
Tadpole into the gilded toad, and brings
Into the midst of frogs unnumbered—frogs
Croaking with newfound voice—a little
Crystalline note or two, fragile and brittle...
The cat sleeps... My Dickette tends to a dog's
Affairs—by day, by night—as sun and moon,
Speckling their heads, rain flecks of light atop them.
And, should rain fall in fact, thick drops festoon
About twig-fingers, green, spread out to stop them.

A linden tree, bamboo... A poet's shelter,
Green... Understand? Yes, green, lest we
Find anything in all that spreading welter
Of grass, moss, tree... Anything that might be
Cruel to old houses, or do injury
To their tired eyes! "Solitude"... As time wings
Along, can there be any living things
More alive than a garden—ever blooming,
Lush and mysterious, obstinate, perfuming
The air, so full of creatures living there
That we chat with a thousand genies, looming—
Aladdin-like—from who knows how or where?

A green word... Who can tell the infinite
Colors of sap, and source, and air in it,
Bathing your house, that timeless go-between
Shielding you from the universe? For some,
Just a dry desert-word, boring, humdrum...
For you, an island refuge, tender... Green...

Des Livres? Soit...

Des livres? Soit. Mais en hiver.
Que le jardin soit gris, la vitre grise!
Que la brise, dehors, soit de la bise
Et la chaleur, dedans, celle de tisons clairs.

Des livres... Mais un ciel de Londres
Et des larmes sur les carreaux, en train de fondre...

Manteaux sentant le vétyver,
Chats en boule, manchons, marrons—l'hiver!

Alors, si vous voulez, un livre—pas des livres—
Un seul, mais beau comme le printemps vert,
L'été doré, le rouge automne grand ouvert,
Plein d'oisillons bavards et de papillons ivres!

Lequel m'offrirez-vous, lequel
M'apportera cela, demain, père Noël?

Des images, bien sûr... C'est le temps des images.
Saluons-nous, Bergers, Rois Mages!
Et des contes... Bonjour, prince Charmant!
Et de l'histoire... que je vois, mais autrement.
Et des voyages... que me gâtent les naufrages!
Père Noël, père Noël, ne cachez-vous
Dans votre hotte, un brin de houx,
Dans votre barbe, un grain de givre?

Ne remplaceraient-ils ce gros livre, entre nous?
Mon livre à moi n'est pas un livre,
Comme ceux qu'on imprime, et, jusqu'au bout,
Vos feuillets bien coupés, je ne pourrais les suivre.

Books? Fine...

Books? Fine... But only in December's
Winter-gray days. The garden, gray...
The window, gray. Outside, a howling day.
Inside, the warmth of glowing embers.

Books... Only under London skies, and rains
Rolling tears down the weeping window panes...

Cloaks with a whiff of fragrant clime,
Cats in a ball, muffs, chestnuts... Wintertime!

So, if you must, a book—not books, just one!—
Green as the spring, gold as the summer sun
And open wide in its red autumn guise
With twittering birds and drunken butterflies!

You'll give me one tomorrow. Who can tell
Which one you're going to bring me, Père Noël?

Pictures? Yes, it's that season. Generously...
Greetings, you Shepherds and you Wise Men Three!
And tales... Prince Charming, I bid you good day!
And history... But told my special way!
And travels... Oh! How shipwrecks trouble me!
Père Noël, don't you have a sprig
Of holly in your sack? The merest twig?
And, in your beard, a drop of frosty dew?

Well, frankly, *entre nous*, wouldn't all that
Be better than some volume, big and fat?
My book's not like those books you read straight through—
Pages all neatly cut—that make no sense.

On ne lit pas un conte... On s'en souvient.
Je l'écoute, brodé par les flammes dansantes.
Ceux qu'on ne me dit pas, je les invente!

L'Histoire? Un conte aussi. Pour les voyages, rien,
Rien, sachez-le, ne me retient
Si quelque oiseau bleu me fait signe.

Quant aux poèmes... soit. Nous attendrons l'été.
L'été n'a pas besoin de rimes qui s'alignent.
Attendons seulement le pourpre velouté
De cette rose que je sais, près de la vigne...

(Décembre 1925)

Premières feuilles

Vous vous tendez vers moi, vertes petites mains des arbres,
Vertes petites mains des arbres du chemin.
Pendant que les vieux murs un peu plus se délabrent,
Que les vieilles maisons montrent leurs plaies,
Vous vous tendez vers moi, bourgeons des haies,
Verts petits doigts.

Petits doigts en coquilles,
Petits doigts jeunes, lumineux, pressés de vivre,
Par-dessus les vieux murs vous vous tendez vers nous.
Le vieux mur dit: "Gare au vent fou,
Gare au soleil trop vif, gare aux nuits qui scintillent,
Gare à la chèvre, à la chenille,
Gare à la vie, ô petits doigts!"

Tales are to be recalled, not read... I call
One to mind as flames dance, embroider all
About it... Those untold, my mind invents!

History? Tales as well... And travels? No,
Nothing prevents me. Off I go
When blue bird summons me to wander hence.

And poems?... Fine. But wait for summer, do!
It has no need of rhyming, line by line.
Wait only for that rose of crimson hue
And velvet petal, blooming by the vine...

(December 1925)

First Leaves

You reach your little tree-green hands to me,
Little green hands of trees lined orderly.
The old walls crumble, wounds are seen
Scarring the aging houses, yet you reach
Your hedge-hands to my fingers, each to each.
Your little fingers green.

Little shell-fingers, young,
Luminous, eager, hurrying to grow...
You reach over the old walls spread below.
An old wall says: "Beware wild gusts, beware
The sun, burning unstrung.
Beware the night twinkling the air.
Beware the goat, the caterpillar's tongue...
Beware life, little fingers green!"

Verts petits doigts griffus, bourrus et tendres,
Vous sentez bien pourquoi
Les vieux murs, ce matin, ont la voix de Cassandre.
Petits doigts en papier de soie,
Petits doigts de velours ou d'émail qui chatoie,
Vous savez bien pourquoi
Vous n'écouterez pas les murs couleur de cendre...

Frêles éventails verts, mains du prochain été,
Nous sentons bien pourquoi vous n'écoutez
Ni les vieux murs, ni les toits qui s'affaissent;
Nous savons bien pourquoi
Par-dessus les vieux murs, de tous vos petits doigts,
Vous faites signe à la jeunesse.

Le Chemin des arbres

I. LE CHEMIN DU CÈDRE

J'ai rencontré le cèdre
Nous nous sommes tous deux reconnus. Il m'a dit:
"C'est toi, toi que je sais, dont les bras sont enduits
de ma résine blanche et dont les cheveux brillent
de mes fines aiguilles
et dont les poches craquent
de mes pommes de cèdre..."

Je n'ai rien dit.
Mais son odeur à lui,
d'encens, d'ambre et de cèdre,
est bien ce que je sais comme il sait tout le reste.

Fingers, like rough or tender claws this morning,
How well you know what those walls mean.
Cassandra-voiced, they warn you. But what for?
Tissue-like fingers, or
Velveted, or enameled, shimmering green—
How well you know why you ignore
Those ashen-colored walls and all their warning...

Frail little fans of green,
Hands of next summer's heat,
How well we know why you eschew
Those crumbling roofs and the old walls effete:
Over the walls, it's youth that you
Are reaching to...

The Trees' Path

I. THE CEDAR'S PATH

I happened on the cedar there.
We recognized each other, and he said:
"Yes, I know you're the one whose arms are spread
with my white resin, and whose hair
shines with my needles fine,
whose pockets crackle,
full of those cedar-cones of mine..."

I hold my tongue.
But there, among
his cedar scents—incense and amber smell—
is what I know and all he knows as well.

II. LE CHEMIN DU CHÊNE

J'ai rencontré le chêne,
le vieux chêne aux abeilles.
Il a toujours le coeur ouvert, mais moins d'abeilles,
moins de miel semble-t-il au fond de son coeur noir.
Des essaims l'ont quitté peut-être—
ou j'ai passé trop tard ce soir.
Le chêne secouait sa vieille tête
comme un homme bien seul...

III. LE CHEMIN DE L'ORMEAU

J'ai rencontré l'ormeau.
Pas un ormeau célèbre,
mais un ormeau sans ex-voto,
tournant le dos à la route des hommes.

Sa colonne de bois, rugueuse, nue, énorme,
quelqu'un l'a-t-il jamais serrée entre ses bras?
Nous l'avions mesurée avec un fil de soie
la colonne de bois qui ne s'arrête pas
de grossir en silence.

Mais grossir—qui jamais voit grossir un ormeau?
Tant de jours et de nuits, tant de soleil et d'eau,
de paix, d'oubli, de chance... tant et tant!
Entre les émondeurs, les chenilles, l'autan,
j'ai rencontré la Patience.

IV. LE CHEMIN DES GENÉVRIERS

J'ai retrouvé mes petits genévriers,
tordus, piquants roussis, cramponnés aux rochers
comme des acrobates.
Ah! le bleu d'outremer de leurs petites baies
le long des couchants écarlates!

II. THE OAK TREE'S PATH

I happened on the oak tree there,
the old oak with his bees.
His heart stands open still, but fewer bees,
and far less honey in his dark heart too.
Swarms must have left him—so it might
appear—or I've come passing through
perhaps a little late tonight.
He shook his old head like a lonely man...

III. THE YOUNG ELM'S PATH

I happened on the young elm there.
No special elm with an ex-voto prayer,
just a plain elm that turned his back, ignored
the road that men go walking on.

His trunk: a wooden pillar—rough, thick, bare.
Had it ever been hugged, embraced? Once we
measured it round with silken cord
this wooden pillar, and would look
as it grew silently.

"Grew" did I say? Does anyone
watch an elm grow? Day after day, rain, sun,
nights, calm neglect... With not a little luck,
grown thick, despite gales, insects, pruning-hook...
Patience is what I happened on.

IV. THE JUNIPERS' PATH

I've come across my junipers again—
Small, snarled, and ruddy-thorned—clinging, like men
in acrobatic pose, outspread
against the rocks. Their berries' deep-sea blue
stands out against the sunset's scarlet red!

Ils se hérissent, ronds ou si déchiquetés
que tout le ciel traverse
leurs petits corps fantasques.
Le gazon ras joue au tapis de Perse
mais le vent s'y jette en bourrasque.

Ici, les lièvres et les chèvres
échappent aux hommes d'en bas.
Ici bleuissent les genièvres
pour l'oiseau que l'on ne voit pas.

Petit grain bleu, sauvage, amer,
semé parmi les toisons rousses
d'arbres nains que l'hiver rebrousse
comme les oursins dans la mer.

V. LE CHEMIN DU ROSEAU

Puis j'ai rencontré le roseau,
le roseau vert qui dit: "Je plie et ne romps pas."
Les pieds dans l'eau,
il se courbait si bas
que ses rubans encombraient le ruisseau.
Il avait oublié son âme de pipeau.

Son front vert saluait, saluait sans relâche,
son dos se balançait comme un dos de serpent
et jamais le soleil ne le voyait en face.

Il disait aux pipas:
"Je plie et ne romps pas, je plie et ne romps pas..."
enfin, ce qu'il disait au chêne
de Monsieur Jean de La Fontaine.

Et l'âne qui broutait l'a brouté tout de même.

• • •

Je n'ai pas rencontré le baobab.

They bristle, a round mass, or twist and shred
that lets the whole vast sky come lighting through
their curious little shapes. The ground, clip-grassed,
thinks it's a Persian carpet, but a blast
of wind comes whirling round and brings it to.

Up here the hare and goat roam free
of man below. And up here these
berries put on their blue, to be
food for the bird that no one sees.

Little blue berries—wild and bitter—sown
among the dwarf-trees, reddened fleecily,
trees tousled by the winter winds, tossed, thrown
about like spiny urchins in the sea...

V. THE REED'S PATH

And then I happened on the reed—
Young, green—a reed that said: "You know,
I bend but never break..." So low
he bowed, feet in the water, that, indeed.
his ribbons tousled and got tangled.
And, his reed soul forgotten, there he dangled...

His green brow nodded, nodded, never ending,
and, like a snake, his back, crooking and bending,
turned from the sun, who never saw his face.

He told the toads: "You know... You know...
I bend but never break..." Ah so...
Saying what once he told the oak, again—
the oak of Monsieur Jean de La Fontaine.

Grazing, the ass grazed on him nonetheless.

• • •

I didn't happen on the baobab.

Vigne vierge d'automne

Vous laissez tomber vos mains rouges,
Vigne vierge, vous les laissez tomber
Comme si tout le sang du monde était sur elles.

A leur frisson, toute la balustrade bouge,
Tout le mur saigne,
O vigne vierge... Tout le ciel est imbibé
D'une même lumière rouge.

C'est comme un tremblement d'ailes rouges qui tombent,
D'ailes d'oiseaux des îles, d'ailes
Qui saignent. C'est la fin d'un règne
Ou quelque chose de plus simple infiniment.

Ce sont les pieds palmés de hauts flamants
Ou de fragiles pattes de colombes
Qui marchent dans l'allée.
Où vont-elles, si rouges?
Leurs traces étoilées
Rejoignent l'autre vigne, où l'on vendange.

Si rouge,
Est-ce déjà le sang des cuves pleines?
Ah! simplement la fête des vendanges,
Simplement n'est-ce pas?

Et pourtant, que vos mains sont tremblantes! Leurs veines
Se rompent une à une... Tant de sang...
Et cette odeur si fade, étrange.
Ces mains qui tombent d'un air las,
O vigne vierge, d'un air las et comme absent,
Ces mains abandonnées...

Autumn's Creeping Vine

You let your hands fall to the ground,
Your red hands, creeping vine... You let them fall
As if all of the earth's blood weighed them down.

The railing feels them flutter past, the wall
Bleeds with a reddish brown,
O creeping vine... And the whole sky is full
Of the same color's light all round.

Like a red shuddering of falling wings—
Island-bird's wings—they shed
Their blood. And so a reign is dead,
Or one of those even much simpler things.

Webbed feet of tall flamingos, or
Doves' fragile feet, pattering down the lane...
(Where are they headed for,
So red?) Their star-like prints
Approach the other vine, where harvesting's
Tasks have begun, long since...

So red...
Is it the blood of vats already full?
Ah! Just the harvest feast! No more
Than that! No more, I said...

And yet, look at your trembling hands! Each vein,
One at a time, bursts... So much blood,
And that odd smell, so drab, so dull.
Those hands that fall, weary, each one,
O creeping vine—oblivious, undone,
Hands left for lost...

Lady Macbeth n'eut-elle pas ce geste
Après avoir frotté la tache si longtemps?

Mains qui se crispent, mains qui restent
En lambeaux rouges sur octobre palpitant;
Dites, oh! dites chaque année
Etes-vous les mains meurtrières de l'Automne?

Ou chaque année,
Sans rien qui s'en émeuve ni personne,
Des mains assassinées
Qui flottent au fil rouge de l'automne?

L'Heure du platane

Sentez-vous cette odeur, cette odeur fauve et rousse
de beau cuir neuf, chauffé par l'automne qui flambe?

Tous les cuirs du Levant sont là, venus ensemble
de souks lointains saturés d'ambre et de santal.
Des huiles et des gommes d'or les éclaboussent.

En de jaunes parfums d'essences et de gousses,
tous les cuirs précieux d'un faste oriental,
cuirs gaufrés et gravés, pointillés de métal,
peints et damasquinés, sont là. Ceux de Cordoue
s'allongent en panneaux où la lumière joue
comme dans l'escalier d'un *palacio* ducal;
ceux de Russie ont des reflets de pourpre ardente;
ceux de Venise la douceur d'épais velours,
et ceux des Flandres aux blonds rares, aux bruns sourds,
semblent chez le bourgmestre attendre une kermesse.

Did Lady Macbeth not make that gesture too,
To rub the stain clean? Trying... Trying...

Hands clenched, shreds of red hands laid crossed
On an October bosom lying,
Gasping: the hands that kill the Autumn, dying
Year after year?... Are you? Are you?

Or hands that, every year, time-tossed,
Are slain—no fuss and no ado,
And none to care!—and that go floating, dead,
Along the autumn's trickling stream of red?

The Plane Tree Hour

Can you smell that red, tawny scent, that scent
of fine new leather warmed with autumn's flame?

Leathers of the Levant together came
from distant markets, dripping, redolent
with amber, sandalwood, gold oils, spiced gum.

Fragrant with gilded cloves, with cardamom,
costliest leathers from the Orient,
embossed, sharp awl-engraved and opulent,
tinted and damasked... And they all lie there—
Cordovan too—spread on the *étagère,*
bright in the light, like a magnificent
staircase in some ducal *palacio...*
The Russian ones, burnished with crimson glow;
the ones from Venice, soft, thick-velveted;
from Flanders—seldom blond, dull-dark of head—
seem to wait for the burgomeister's fair.

Quelles mains ont offert à ces livres de messe
la reliure somptueuse qui m'enchante?
Et ce manteau pareil à la robe de Dante,
qui le tailla pour des poètes ignorés?

Beaux livres d'autrefois, je vous aime, dorés
sur un fond de soleil ainsi que des Icones,
et ma bibliothèque est en gala d'automne
ce soir, entre les bras d'un arbre mitré d'or.

La légende se brode à même le décor.
Mes livres, des très vieux aux très jeunes, s'étagent
de branche en branche, à la façon d'oiseaux pensifs,
et par-dessus la mosaïque des massifs
prennent la gamme fauve et rousse du feuillage.

Car ils sont habillés de feuilles, en ce temps
où les platanes roux et fauves se dépouillent.
La vierge, dans l'allée, a filé sa quenouille
afin que chaque page ait un signet flottant.

Vous qui lisez, le front penché, dans une chambre,
ne sentez-vous donc pas qu'au seuil froid de novembre
tout ce maroquin neuf et ces parchemins d'or
sont faits pour que, ce soir, on traduise, dehors,
uniquemnt, les strophes du platane? Automne,
guilloché de soleil, broché d'insectes jaunes,
plein de miel et de grains, et de cette odeur forte
que promène le vent du sud, de porte en porte;

Automne, qui donc pourrait croire aux feuilles mortes,
croire, ce soir, à la tristesse de la mort?

What hands have crafted for these missals such
a lavish binding, sumptuous to the touch?
Who tailored this fine cloak, as richly sewn
as Dante's, for these poets now unknown?

Yesterday's books! I love you tenderly,
like Icons on a field of sun, gilt-set
in the embrace of a gold-mitered tree.
Tonight my bookshelf sports an autumn *fête:*
legend stitched on the setting's fantasy.

My books—some very old, some young—lie spread
like pensive birds, from branch to branch, perched there
above the plateaus' rich mosaic, where
the foliage turns them shades of tawny red.

They wear the leaves now fallen from the trees
as plane trees, red and tawny, strip their clothes.
The virgin's spindle, in the lane, comes, goes,
spinning each page a bookmark in the breeze.

You, reading in your room, head bowing low,
don't you know, at November's chill threshold,
that all that new Morocco, all that old
gold parchment, has been fashioned only so
that those plane trees, out there, this night, might be
translated? Autumn. Sun-whorled bindings, sewn
with yellow-insect thread, hung heavily
with grains and honey, and that smell, gust-blown
from door to door, the southwind's pungent breath...

Autumn. Who can believe leaves die? Can we
believe, this night, in sadness unto death?

Diégo

Son nom est de là-bas, comme sa race.
L'oeil vif, le pas dansant, les cheveux noirs,
C'est un petit cheval des sierras, qui, le soir,
Longtemps, regarde vers le sud, humant l'espace.

Il livre toute sa crinière au vent qui passe
Et, près de son oreille, on cherche le pompon
D'un oeillet rouge. Sur son front,
Ses poils frisent, pareils à de la laine.

Rien en lui de ces chevaux minces qui s'entraînent
Le long d'un champ jalonné de poteaux;
Ni rien du lourd cheval né dans les plaines,
Ces plaines grasses et luisantes de canaux
Où des chalands s'en vont avec un bruit de chaînes.

Il ignore le turf, et les charrois et les labours,
Celui dont le pied sûr comme celui des chèvres,
Suivit là-haut les sentiers bleus, dans les genièvres.

Sur ses naseaux, larges ouverts, un frisson court.
Avec d'autres poulains échevelés, il vint, un jour,
De la montagne aux herbes odorantes.
Poussé par des bergers en capes de brigands
Il vint, petit cheval hirsute à crinière flottante...

Il a gardé ses yeux surpris, des yeux d'enfant
Qui fixent loin, comme à travers les choses...

Et parfois on y voit luire un éclair, sans cause.
On dit alors... "Vient-il de Corse?" Mais il a
D'autres regards aussi, pleins de tendresse.
La jument du vieux cheik a de ces regards-là
Pour le maître en burnous qu'elle aime. "Une caresse
Fait l'antilope et le cheval de la maison."

Diégo

His name, just like his race, comes from down there.
Sparkling of eye, sprightly of pace, mane black,
Little sierra horse, who gazes back
Nightly—long, southward gaze!—sniffing the air.

With passing winds he tosses and unfurls
His hair.... A pompom there, carnation-red,
By his ear; and, atop his head
And brow, woollen-like, little tufts of curls.

Nothing is there about him like those slim
Steeds that for racecourse rivalries are bred.
Nor is there robust dray horse breed in him,
Born of the plains bright with canals, whose chains
And ropes resound, hauling now fro, now to...

He knows no turf, no plough, no wagon-reins,
He who, on high, sure-hoofed on paths of blue
Juniper, picks his steps as goats can do.

His nostrils wide flare with a breathy neigh.
He came with other frisky colts one day,
From sweet-grass mountain top to me.
Brigand-caped shepherds urged him on his way—
My little horse, mane flowing, blowing free...

And still he keeps his far-off look, those eyes
Like a child's, staring, gazing in surprise...

Sometimes one sees a sudden flash, though for
No cause, and asks: "Is he a Corsican?"
But he has other looks as well, far more
Heartfelt; like those the old equestrian
Sheik's mare gives her burnoosed, belovèd master,
"Whose soft caress turns her at once—or faster—
To bounding antelope or household horse."

Pas un tournant d'allée, un morceau de gazon,
Une porte d'ici qu'il ne connaisse...

Et les portes peuvent s'ouvrir imprudemment.
Le petit cheval noir y secoue, un moment,
Sa tête qui dit: "Non, pourquoi fuirais-je?"
Il hennit comme on rit, à mi-voix, en arpège;
Et sa queue, ainsi qu'un éventail,
S'agite avec le bruit de feuillages qu'on traîne.

Il connaît chaque route au delà du portail,
Et peut-être sait-il où chaque route mène.

Se prêtant au harnais, par jeu, derrière lui
Il a tiré parfois cette chose qui bouge—
Une voiture—et fait tinter le collier rouge
Dont les grelots ont le son de clarines dans la nuit.

Parfois, comme pris de folie,
On le voit bondissant pour rien, pour un peu d'eau,
Un jet de l'arroseur ou trois gouttes de pluie,
Un papier tournoyant, et ses petits sabots
Allument le pavé. Parfois, dans le pré, libre,
Il se met à ruer d'un air farouche, exprès!
Il galope en zigzags, ou, pliant les jarrets,
Se tient debout, nous défiant, en équilibre...

Quand on le mène boire, il saisit, par un coin,
Nos tabliers, nos manches, ce qu'il peut, et nous dirige,
Lui, le petit cheval sans bride. Un brin de foin
Pend de sa lèvre brune—ou quelque tige
Arrachée au vieux mur—et son oeil songe, au loin...

No path, no turn, no sprig of gorse,
No blade of grass, no door he does not know...

And if the doors stand open, thoughtlessly,
My little black horse shakes his head, and he
Whinnies arpeggios in a laughing "Oh?
Why should I flee? No, no!..." And he will flail
The air, sweeping the twigs with fan-like tail.

He knows each road beyond the gate. And I
Suspect he knows where each one leads as well.

And he will not object when, by and by,
Harnessed, he has to drag—mere bagatelle!—
That moving thing behind him that they call
A "wagon"; and his collar, red, with all
Its jingling tinkling, like cowbells at night.

At times, as if gone mad, he might
Leap at some trifle... Water... Raindrops, two
Or three... The garden-hose's spray... A few
Paper scraps in the breeze, in twisting flight.
Then will his little hooves light up the ground!
At other times, free as you please, he goes
With fearsome air, darting here, there, all round,
Zigzagging... Or, rearing up tall, he throws
His forepaws high, strikes a defiant pose...

And when we water him, often he takes
Our sleeves, our aprons in his teeth, and makes
Us follow where he leads, though bridleless...
A wisp of hay—or a stem that he rips
From the old wall—hangs dangling from his lips,
As, gazing off afar, he dreams... Ah, yes...

Voici longtemps, longtemps, bien des années,
Qu'il est de la maison, le petit cheval noir
Dont le poil, fil à fil, en bouclettes fanées,
S'argente sur le front. Il se plaît à nous voir,
A nous porter, à nous conduire. Il nous appelle
Et nous taquine et reste jeune et reste gai...

Pourtant, quand le vent vient du sud, battant des ailes
Comme un aigle de la Sierra, quand le printemps
A ce parfum de romarin qui nous étonne,
Et tous les soirs, et tous les soirs d'été, d'automne,
Qu'attend-il, mon petit cheval aux yeux d'enfant,
De quoi se souvient-il qui nous étonne,
Quand le vent vient du sud?

La Vieille Femme de la lune

On a beaucoup parlé dans la chambre, ce soir.
Couché, bordé, la lune entrant par la fenêtre,
On évoque à travers un somnolent bien-être,
La vieille qui, là-haut, porte son fagot noir.

Qu'elle doit être lasse et qu'on voudrait connaître
Le crime pour lequel nous pouvons tous la voir
Au long des claires nuits cheminer sans espoir!

Pauvre vieille si vieille, est-ce un vol de bois mort
Qui courbe son vieux dos sur la planète ronde?
Elle a très froid, qui sait, quand le vent souffle fort.
Va-t-elle donc marcher jusqu'à la fin du monde?

Et pourquoi dans le ciel la traîner jusqu'au jour!
On dort... Nous fermerons les yeux à double tour...
Lune, laisse-la donc s'asseoir une seconde.

For years he's been—such a long, long time now—
Part of our family, our little pet,
Whose fading curls are silvering his black brow,
Hair by hair. How he loves us when we let
Him bear us horseback, or tug us behind.
He neighs, teases us impishly... And yet,

When winds blow from the south—free, unconfined—
Wings flapping like a Sierra eagle... When
Spring, with its rosemary, wafts once again
To our surprise... And when summer-night skies
Return—and autumn too—what does he then,
This horse of ours, he of the childlike eyes...
Just what does he recall, to our surprise,
When winds blow from the south?

The Old Woman in the Moon

Tucked in... Tonight a lot of bedroom chatter...
The moon slips through the window; on her back
The old crone hauls her sheaves of firewood, black,
As in a drowsing calm we wonder at her.

How weary she must be beneath her pack!
What crime was hers, that—hopeless, till the crack
Of dawn—she roams the night? What was the matter?

Poor soul, so old! Was it her theft? Was it
For some dead twigs that she bows, bending low
On planet round? And when the chill gusts blow,
Must she plod on, eternal, infinite?

Why drag her through the sky till day's first light?
Sleep, now... We close our eyes and lock them tight.
Moon, let the poor thing sit and rest a bit.

Le Cinéma

Pour un vieux monsieur
qui ne comprend pas le cinéma

Trou d'ombre. Grotte obscure, où l'on sent, vaguement,
Bouger des êtres. La pâleur de l'écran nu
Comme une baie ouverte, au fond, sur l'inconnu...
Musique en sourdine, tiédeur, chuchotements,
Odeur de mandarine,
De sucre d'orge et d'amandes grillées.
Attente, carillon d'un timbre qui s'obstine,
Petite danse de lueurs éparpillées.

Puis, coup de soleil brusque. Le mystère
De ce carré de neige s'animant.
Floraisons de jardins, pics, fleuves, coins charmants,
Coins tragiques, villes, forêts, la vaste terre...
La vaste terre, et le ciel vaste, et la magie
De visages parlant des yeux, des lèvres,
Sans la voix.

Gestes précis, calme, énergie
Ou nerfs qui cèdent, fièvres,
Bonheurs et désespoirs... des paroles, pourquoi?
Un sourire, une larme,
Un battement de cils...
L'émotion n'est pas dans le vacarme.
Une ligne, des points... voici le fil
Du roman triste ou gai qui se déroule.

Aimes-tu voir les hommes s'agiter?
Assis, tu regardes la foule.

The Cinema

For an old gentleman
who doesn't understand the cinema

Dark cavern, grotto where, vaguely, you feel
People moving about, unreal.
The warmth, the muted music, whisperings...
And, like a bay open to unknown things,
The naked screen's
Blank pallor. Barley-sugar smell,
And tangerines,
And almonds roasting. And the warning bell
Stubbornly ringing to a glittering dance.

Then, sudden burst of sun... Mysterious,
That snow-white square that comes to life, enchants:
Gardens in bloom, peaks, glorious
Or piteous places, rivers, and no dearth
Of cities, forests, all the whole vast earth...
Vast earth, vast sky... The sorcery
Of talking faces, moving lips, mute speech,
Eloquent eye.

Calm air or fevered gestures. Agony,
Hope, or despair. Nerves tense, that reach
The silent breaking-point... Words? Why?
A smile, a tear,
A fluttering lash...
Emotion needs no clattering clash.
A story line, a point or two... And here
The tale unfolds. Happy or sad, so be it.

Would you see men dash recklessly?
Look at the crowds and you will see it

Aimes-tu le désert? Tu le parcours, l'été,
Sous un torrent de feu, sans autre peine
Que de laisser pour toi marcher les sables... Plaines,
Montagnes, mers, te livrent leurs secrets
Et le pôle est si près
Que Nanouk l'Esquimau t'accueille en frère;
Et la jungle est si près
Que tu t'en vas avec le chasseur de panthères...
O beaux voyages que jamais tu ne ferais!

Tous les héros, tu les connais,
Ceux de l'Histoire et ceux de la légende;
Tous les contes des Mille et une nuits,
Les contes d'autrefois, ceux d'aujourd'hui
Et les temples, et les palais,
Et les vieux bourgs où les clairs de lune descendent...
Tu les connais... Tu les connais, toi, prisonnier,
Peut-être, de murs gris, de choses grises, toi
Dont la vie est grise ou pire...

Vois, des fleurs s'ouvrent, des oiseaux t'invitent, vois:
Aux vergers d'Aladin s'emplissent des paniers...
Cueille des rêves, toi qui fus un prisonnier!
Ainsi qu'une arche de porphyre,
La muraille s'écarte.... Evade-toi!
Il pleut—ou le vent souffle sur le toit,
Ou c'est juillet qui brûle, ou dans la rue,
C'est trop dimanche avec trop de gens qui bavardent—
Viens dans ce petit coin merveilleux et regarde...

While you sit calmly as can be!
Is the desert your pleasure? You
Have but to let the sands of time flow free,
And, with no pain or how-d'ye-do,
Cross it in summer's fires torrential... Seas,
Mountains, and plains reveal their mysteries.
And the North Pole is so
Close to you that Nanouk the Eskimo
Welcomes you as his brother, as his kin.
And the jungle is so
Close to you that you'll even want to go
Off with the panther hunter, risk your skin...
O travel rare, and never to be done!

You know the heroes, every one,
The real, the legendary: every story—
A Thousand and One Nights—tales of the past
And of today as well: palaces vast,
Temples shining in all their glory,
Old town bathed in the moonlight's glow... Ah yes,
You know... You know them all... Pent futureless
In your gray prison ... Gray walls... Everything
Gray... You, whose life is one gray nothingness.

Look! Birds invite you! Buds are blossoming.
Aladdin's gardens, baskets brimming... Come
Pick out your dreams... Flee from your prison! See?
It stands like ark of porphyry,
Gates wide. Today, no wearisome
Weather: tempest or torrent, torrid heat
Of Sunday in July... And, in the street—
Too much a Sunday!—people spin,
Sputter their endless chatter. Come, go in...
Sit in this wondrous place... Open your eyes...

Ici, l'heure vécue,
Même terrible—tous les drames sont possibles—
N'est qu'à demi terrible,
Et te voilà, comme les tout-petits,
Riant, toi qui pleurais... Tu ris,
Toi, vieux comme les écoliers que rien n'étonne.

Charlie est là... Charlie! Et Keaton, et Rimsky.
Et pour ce bon rire, conquis
Sur toi-même, c'est le meilleur d'eux-mêmes
Qu'ils te donnent.

Art muet, soit... N'ajoute rien. Tu l'aimes,
Tu l'aimeras, quoi que tu dises, l'art vivant
Qui t'offre son visage neuf et son langage,
Ses ralentis, ses raccourcis, tous ses mirages,
Tous ses décors mouvants...
Près de ces gens qui, dans l'ombre, s'effacent,
Viens seulement t'asseoir, veux-tu, sans parti pris?
De la nuit d'une salle étroite, aux longs murs gris,
Regarde ce miracle: un film qui passe...

An hour spent here in fright—
Life's dramas, after all!—shocks, terrifies
Half as much as outside.
Though first you sobbed and cried
Like a mere tot, now there
You sit and laugh, with your smug student air.

Charlie is there, and Keaton, Rimsky too,
Eager to draw that laugh from you
Despite yourself—distrustful of it.
And so they do.

Silent art... Say no more. Yet how you love it
And always will, say what you please. It lives
Life's changing scenes—now fast, now slow. Its pace,
Its rhythm, speaks a novel language, gives
Everything a new, moving face...
Come to the narrow, gray-walled room, and sit
There in the dark, with others, yet alone!
With open mind, come sense the awe of it,
The miracle... A film is being shown...

La Paix

Comment je l'imagine?
Eh bien, je ne sais pas...
Peut-être enfant, très blonde, et tenant dans ses bras
Des branches de glycine?

Peut-être plus petite encore, ne sachant
Que sourire et jaser dans un berceau penchant
Sous les doigts d'une vieille femme qui fredonne...

Parfois, je la crois vieille aussi... Belle, pourtant,
De la beauté de ces Madones
Qu'on voit dans les vitraux anciens. Longtemps—
Bien avant les vitraux—elle fut ce visage
Incliné sur la source, en un bleu paysage
Où les dieux grecs jouaient de la lyre, le soir.

Mais à peine un moment venait-elle s'asseoir
Au pied des oliviers, parmi les violettes,
Bellone avait tendu son arc... Il fallait fuir.
Elle a tant fui, la douce forme qu'on n'arrête
Que pour la menacer encore et la trahir!

Depuis que la terre est la terre
Elle fuit... Je la crois donc vieille et n'ose plus
Toucher au voile qui lui prête son mystère.
Est-elle humaine? J'ai voulu
Voir un enfant aux prunelles si tendres!

Où? Quand? Sur quel chemin faut-il l'attendre
Et sous quels traits la reconnaîtront-ils
Ceux qui, depuis toujours, l'habillent de leur rêve?
Est-elle dans le bleu de ce jour qui s'achève
Ou dans l'aube du rose avril?

Peace

How do I see it? Ah!
Who knows? In my mind's eye,
Perhaps a tow-head tot, her arms piled high
With branches of wisteria?

Or, perhaps, even smaller still:
A smiling infant, blabbering her fill
And cradled by a rocking, humming crone...

Sometimes I see it old as well... But fair,
Beautiful as those dear Madonnas, shown
In old stained glass. Before—long before there
Were even stained-glass windows!—one would see
Her lovely head bent low above a spring
In the bucolic blue tranquillity,
Where Greek gods strummed their lyres, come evening.

But scarcely by the olive trees would she
Sit for a moment, midst the violets, when
Bellona drew her bow... And off, away
This tender soul would flee... Again, again...
Harassed by those intent but to betray!

And so, since earth is earth, she flees...
Grown old, she dares not touch the veil that wraps
Her round, concealed in its deep mysteries.
Is she even a human being? Perhaps.
A child, I might have hoped, with soulful eyes!

When? Where? On what road ought we wait for her?
What will she look like? Will they recognize
Her features, they who ever were
Clothing her in their dreams? Does she prefer
Blue dusk to April morning's pink, reborn?

Ecartant les blés mûrs, paysanne aux mains brunes,
Sourit-elle au soldat blessé?
Comment la voyez-vous, pauvres gens harassés,
Vous, mères qui pleurez, et vous, pêcheurs de lune?

Est-elle retournée aux bois sacrés,
Aux missels fleuris de légendes?
Dort-elle, vieux Corot, dans tes brouillards dorés?
Dans les tiens, couleur de lavande,
Doux Puvis de Chavannes? dans les tiens,
Peintre des Songes gris, mystérieux Carrière?
Ou s'épanouit-elle, Henri Martin, dans ta lumière?

Et puis, je me souviens...
Un son de flûte pur, si frais, aérien,
Parmi des accords lents et graves; la sourdine
De bourdonnants violoncelles vous berçant
Comme un océan calme; une cloche passant.
Un chant d'oiseau, la Musique divine,
Cette musique d'une flotte qui jouait,
Une nuit, dans le chaud silence d'une ville;

Mozart te donnant sa grande âme, paix fragile...
Je me souviens... Mais c'est peut-être, au fond qui sait?
Bien plus simple... Et c'est toi qui la connais,
Sans t'en douter, vieil homme en houppelande,
Vieux berger des sentiers, blonds de genêts,
Cette paix des monts solitaires et des landes,
La paix qui n'a besoin que d'un grillon pour s'exprimer.

Au loin, la lueur d'une lampe ou d'une étoile;
Devant la porte, un peu d'air embaumé...

Peasant, hands tanned, picking the ripening corn,
Does she smile on the wounded soldier lad?
How do you see her, folk forlorn,
You, weeping mothers, and you, sad
Fishermen who would catch the moon?

Has she returned now to the sacred grove?
Into the flowered missals, legend-strewn?
Does she sleep in your gilded-mauve
Mists, old Corot? Or yours, lavender-hued,
Dear Puvis de Chavannes? Or yours, Carrière,
Painter of gray Dream and mysterious mood?
Or bloom, Henri Martin, in your bright air?

And then, from who knows where?...
Suddenly I recall, borne on the breeze,
A flute's fresh and cool notes, pure melodies
Amid the 'cellos' muted chords, drawn long
And low, grumbling, rocking you gently... gently...
Like the calm sea; a passing gong...
Heavenly trills of a bird's sweet song;
Ships' music washing oh so innocently
Over a city's silent heat some night...

Mozart, gifting the fragile peace of his
Great soul... Yes, I recall... Then too, it might
Be simpler still: perhaps it is
Only you, in your shepherd's frock, old man
Who tread the flaxen brushwood pathways, who
Know what it is—although you scarcely can
Suspect that it is you alone who do—
Who know the peace of lonely hill, of thicket
And briar covering the moor, afar...
Peace, blazoned in the chirping of the cricket...

Off in the distance, glimmering lamp or star;
A breath of balm-fresh air before the door...

Comme c'est simple, vois! Qui parlait de tes voiles
Et pourquoi tant de mots pour te décrire? Vois,
Qu'importent les images: maison blanche,
Oasis, arc-en-ciel, angélus, bleus dimanches!
Qu'importe la façon dont chacun porte en soi,
Même sans le savoir, ton reflet qui l'apaise,
Douceur promise aux coeurs de bonne volonté...

Ah! tant de verbes, d'adjectifs, de parenthèses!
Moi qui la sens parfois, dans le jardin, l'été,
Si près de se laisser convaincre et de rester
Quand les hommes se taisent...

So simple, see? What's all this talk of your
Wrapping of veils? And why make such a fuss
Describing you? Just words and words! And why
Those images? The Sundays of blue sky,
The cottage white, rainbows, the angelus,
Oases!... Does it matter, quite, how we—
Each of us—bear, even unknowingly,
The image of the calm that gentles us:
Sweet promised boon to those hearts of good will?

Verbs, adjectives, parentheses!... They fill
The garden air! And there, time and again,
Sometimes, I feel she almost might remain,
Once Man, at last, falls silent, still...

PATHS

Le Chemin des chevaux

N'as-tu pas un cheval blanc
Là-bas dans ton île?
Une herbe sauvage
Croît-elle pour lui?

Ah! comme ses crins flottants
Flottent dans les bras du vent
Quand il se réveille!
Il dort comme un oiseau blanc
Quelque part dans l'île.

J'ai beau marcher dans la rue
Comme tout le monde,
C'est l'herbe, l'herbe inconnue,
Et le cheval chevelu
Couleur de la lune,
Qui sont de chez moi, là-bas,
Dans une île ronde.

Caparaçonnés, au pas, au galop,
Je ne connais pas tes quatre chevaux.

Tu vas à Paris,
La chanson le dit,
Sur ton cheval gris.

Tu vas à La Haye
Sur la jument baie.

Tu vas au manoir
Sur le cheval noir.

Et je ne sais où
Sur le poulain roux.

Mais mon cheval blanc
Nuit et jour m'attend
Au seuil de mon île.

Horses' Path

Don't you have a horse of white
Out there on your isle?
Is the wild grass growing there
For your horse alone?

See the wind's arms in mid-air
Billowing waves of long coarse hair
When the horse awakes!
He sleeps like a white bird there,
Somewhere on your isle.

So I walk the street meanwhile,
Walk, like everyone, in vain :
And the grasses rare, so rare,
And my horse with flowing mane—
Color of the moon—
All come from my land out there,
Roundabout the isle.

Trappings fly, a-gallop or a-trot:
Your fine horses four? I know them not!

To Paris you will go
Riding your horse of gray:
For the song tells us so.

Off to The Hague, away!
Riding your filly bay!

And off to the chateau
Riding your horse of black!

And on your colt's rust back,
Whereto? I do not know!

But mine? My stallion white
Waits for me, day and night,
Just a step from my isle.

Carte postale

Quand l'anémone rouge et les jacinthes bleues
Fleurissent les parcs d'Angleterre,
Une petite fille en robe rouge ou bleue
Descend les escaliers de pierre.

De green, les parterres, le lierre,
Les beaux arbres jamais taillés
Et les sous-bois pleins de jacinthes...

En robe rouge ou bleue—anémone ou jacinthe—
Une petite fille est peinte
Dans le printemps vert et mouillé
De la vieille Angleterre.

Quand j'habitais Florence

Quand j'habitais Florence avec tous mes parents,
Ma mère, ma grand-mère et l'arrière grand-mère
Aux longs cheveux d'argent,
J'aimais tant les iris de nos jardins toscans
Et le parfum de leur terre légère...

Ah! le printemps, depuis, n'est plus un vrai printemps!

Il n'a plus la couleur des vitraux, vos couleurs,
Sainte-Marie-des Fleurs,
Et celles de l'Arno
Sous les ponts recourbés où passait Béatrice.

Postcard

English parks lush with flowers overgrown—
Red hyacinths, blue anemones...
In dress of blue or red, like these,
Little girl coming down the steps of stone...

Flowerbeds, ivy, unpruned trees,
Hyacinths in the underbrush... And green...
Green everywhere, and everything...

In dress of blue or red—like these
Hyacinths and anemones—
Little girl pictured... Lovely scene:
Olde England, green and wet with spring.

When I Lived off in Florence

When I lived off in Florence with my kin—
Mother, Nana, Great-grandmamma as well,
With her long, silver hair—there, in
Our Tuscan gardens, how I loved the spell
Cast by the iris, and earth's airy smell...

Ah! Spring, since then, is not what spring had been!

It wears no more your stained-glass colors, O
Santa Maria dei Fiori, nor
The Arno's, whose arched bridges bore
The steps where Beatrice used to go.

Le soleil qui baignait les salles des Offices
N'a plus cet or subtil de matins déjà chauds
Le long des murs anciens et des champs de repos.

Les rossignols, depuis, ont tous une voix triste
Et l'aube qui persiste
A l'ombre des cyprès, je ne la connais plus.

Nos jardins d'autrefois, nous les avons perdus.

Chemins de l'Est

Quand j'étais Russe, il m'arrivait
de m'appeler Katia, Masha, Tania.
J'avais une niania,
une baba, tout ce qui chante en a
dans les noms russes.
Dans notre isba
Notre-Dame de Portchaïef luisait
comme une étoile et dehors les étoiles
luisaient comme la mosaïque
de notre église à Pâques.
Et sur la terre pâle
de sa pâleur de neige ou rouge
de ses coquelicots, courait comme le vent
mon beau petit cheval de Sibérie.

Traîneaux, bateaux, troupeaux, blanche et rouge Russie,
danses, musique de chez moi, quand j'étais Russe...
Pouvoir de tant souffrir, d'être si vieux, si jeune,
de faire un geste de la main sans pleur ni cri.
J'avais de longues tresses blondes
comme aujourd'hui.

The sun that once bathed the Ufizzi's halls
In subtle morning gold warms us no more
Along the leisure fields and ancient walls.

Since then, the nightingale sings a sad song
And dawning daylight seems all wrong,
Trying to pierce the cypress-shade somehow.

Yesterday's gardens... No, we've lost them now.

Eastern Paths

When I was Russian, sometimes I would be
called Katya, Masha, Tanya.
I had a nyanya,
a baba... all those things that sing in "a"
in Russian names.
And in our isba there,
Our Lady of Portchayoff shone
like a star, and outside the stars
shone like the mosaic
in our church at Easter time.
And running like the wind over the land,
pale as the snow or poppy red,
my handsome little horse come from the Steppes...

Sleighs and sleds, boats, flocks, Russia's reds and whites.
Dances... The music of my land, when I was Russian...
The power to suffer, be so old, so young,
to wave my hand without a tear or shout.
My locks were blond and long,
just like today.

Chemins de l'Ouest

Pour qui vous a-t-on faits, grands chemins de l'Ouest?
Chemins de liberté que l'on suppose tels
et qui mentez sans doute...

Espaces où surgit le Popocatepetl,
où le noir sequoïa cerne d'étranges routes,
où la faune et la flore ont de si vastes ciels
que l'homme ne sait plus à quel étage vivre.
Chemins de liberté que nous supposons libres.

A travers les Pampas court mon cheval sans bride,
mais la ville géante a ses réseaux de feu
et les jeunes mortels faits de toutes les races
ont leurs lassos, leurs murs, leurs pères et leurs dieux.
Des "Trois Puntas" à la mer des Sargasses,
Amériques du Sud, du Nord,
pays des toisons d'or, des mines d'or, de l'or
qui fait l'homme libre et l'esclave
le Pampero peut-être ignore les entraves
et l'aigle boréal, les pièges du chasseur...

Mais, ô ma liberté, plus chère qu'une soeur,
c'est en moi que tu vis, sereine et sédentaire,
pendant que les chemins font le tour de la terre.

Western Paths

Whom did they make you for, great Western paths?
Paths that lead freedomward—or so one dares
suppose, though they would lie...

Where surges Popocatepetl high,
where black sequoias ring strange thoroughfares,
and plants, beasts spread beneath so vast a sky
that man himself lives on what floor? Who knows?
Paths that lead freedomward, free, we suppose...

My horse, unreined, courses the Pampas' spaces,
but the huge city's web of fire bursts forth
and youthful mortals fashioned from all races
have lassos, forebears, gods and walls. Behold,
from the "Tres Puntas" to Sargasso's sea,
Americas—the South, the North—
lands of the golden fleeces, gold mines, gold
that makes a man both slave and free.
The Gaucho knows no fettering bonds, perhaps,
no Boreal eagles and no hunters' traps...

You, dearer than a sister, Liberty,
you live within me... Calm, I sit my ground
as all the while those paths gird the earth round.

Chemins du Nord

Lorsque "je pâlissais au nom de Vancouver"
et que j'étais du Nord,
trop de froid traversait ma pelisse d'hiver
et mon bonnet de bêtes mortes.
Mes frères chassaient les oursons
jusqu'au fond des grottes de fées;
du sang parlait sous leurs trophées,
les Tomtes se cachaient, le vent hurlait aux portes
et la glace barrait les fjords
lorsque j'étais du Nord.
Murs blancs du froid, prison.
Je ne voyais jamais passer Nils Holgerson.

Selma, Selma, pourquoi m'aviez-vous oubliée?
Il fallait naître à Morbacka, le jour de Pâques.
Je savais bien pourtant que j'étais conviée...

Northern Paths

Back when "the name Vancouver turned me pale,"
I was a Northerner:
the winter chill pierced my pelt cape; the gale
blew through my cap of dead-beast fur.
My brothers, deep in fairy grottos, were
hunting for bear cubs. Eloquent,
beneath their trophies, blood lay spent;
the Goblins hid away; the winds rose, fell,
growled at the doors... Again, again...
Ice closed the fjords up tight, back when
I was a Northerner:
walls white with cold, a jail... And I
never did see Nils Holgerson fly by.

Ah! You forgot me, Selma! Why, pray tell?
Would I were born at Morbacka, on Easter Day.
I know I was invited though!... Oh well...

Chemins du Sud

Chemins du Sud avec un nom qui vous fait mal
certains jours
à force de creuser des nostalgies...
Inscrits en rouge ou bleu sur le cristal
de vos grandes agences de voyage,
inscrits sur les navires au mouillage,
sur l'avion postal
ou sur l'oiseau qui craint le froid des jours plus courts,
certains jours—certains jours
comme se fait insidieuse leur magie!

Chemins du Sud—l'odeur du pamplemousse
ou du désert sans oasis
ou de la forêt vierge aux dangereuses nuits.

Pistes de bêtes dans la brousse
ou dans ces mers pleines d'étoiles rousses
dont parlent entre eux les marins.

Soleil du Sud qui fait la peau d'huile et d'ébène,
soirs de villages indigènes,
tam-tam... Plus loin que vous, au Sud,
Bolero de Ravel qui pourtant faites mal
comme ces noms aux tristesses étranges,
bord astral
de ces routes sans ange
où sombre lentement la Croix du Sud...

Southern Paths

Southern paths, with a name that troubles you
on certain days
as you scratch for nostalgia's memories...
Letters on glass, in red or blue,
on those great travel agencies,
or on ships anchored, or upon
the plane that flies the mail, or on
the bird that fears a cold sun's last short rays
on certain days, on certain days,
how subtle is the magic that they do!

Southern paths: scent of grapefruit—heavy, lush—
of arid desert—no oasis, none!—
of virgin forest nights, and dire risks run.

Traces of beasts, tracks in the underbrush,
in starfish-studded sea, stars red of hue
that sailors talk about, typically.

Southern sun, skin turned glistening ebony,
evenings in native black villages spent,
tom-tom... Then farther south... And you,
Ravel's Bolero, you who torment more
and more, with names sad in their curiousness,
the astral shore
of those routes angel-less
where sinks the Southern Cross in slow descent...

Le Chemin du moulin

Embranchement. Le moulin me fait signe.
Ce n'est pas un moulin à vent
Mais ses ailes battent dans l'eau secrètement
Et ses canards sont blancs comme des cygnes.
Ses colombes ont l'air du Saint-Esprit. Son porche
A l'air de précéder une église. Au couchant
Sa fenêtre à meneaux flambe comme une torche.
Il n'a pas d'autre nom que le Moulin, pour le passant.

Le Chemin des veuves

Veuves—tant de veuves si veuves
avec ce nom créé pour elles,
avec ce noir comme une preuve.

Pauvre veuve. On dit: pauvre veuve,
et c'est le malheur en série.
Ah! c'est un Dieu sourd que l'on prie.

Veuve jeune, belle peut-être,
ou vieille et seule un soir de vent.
Ah! cet arbre sous la fenêtre...

On allait dehors deux ensemble.
On savait bien peu l'un de l'autre
mais la prière des Apôtres
brûlait peut-être dans le vent.

Quai désert. Havre dévasté.
Qui peut dire de quel moment
on est veuf pour l'éternité?

The Mill's Path

Fork in the road. The mill beckons to me.
It's not a windmill, but its wings
Shimmer the water with mute flutterings
And ducks as white as swans, doves that could be,
Each one, the Holy Ghost... Its little porch's
Space seems a church-front. Sunset, and the sky,
Torch-like, flares in its mullioned panes—flames, scorches...
"The Mill"... Its only name known to the passerby.

Widows' Path

Widows well-widowed... So many stood
with that name made for them alone,
with that black, proof of widowhood.

Poor widow. Yes, that's what we say,
poor widow, woes strung one by one.
Ah! God is deaf to those who pray.

Widow, young, perhaps lovely still,
or lonely, old, some windy night.
Ah! that tree by the window sill...

Together we would take the air.
We knew each other little, though
the words of the Apostles' prayer
seemed to burn in the windy night.

Abandoned wharf. Harbor laid low,
laid waste... Who knows what moment we
are widowed for all eternity?.

Le Chemin de sable

Ne pas se rappeler en suivant ce chemin...
Ne pas se rappeler... Je te donnais la main.
Nos pas étaient semblables,
Nos ombres s'accordaient devant nous sur le sable,
Nous regardions très loin ou tout près, simplement.
L'air sentait ce qu'il sent en ce moment.
Le vent ne venait pas de l'Océan. De là
Ni d'ailleurs. Pas de vent. Pas de nuage. Un pin
Dont le jumeau fut coupé dans le temps
Etait seul. Nous parlions ou nous ne parlions pas.
Nous passions, mais si sûrs de la belle heure stable!
Ne te retourne pas sur le chemin de sable.

Le Chemin de l'amour

Amour, mon cher amour, je te sais près de moi
Avec ton beau visage.
Si tu changes de nom, d'accent, de cœur et d'âge,
Ton visage du moins ne me trompera pas.
Les yeux de ton visage, amour, ont près de moi
La clarté patiente des étoiles.
De la nuit, de la mer, des îles sans escales,
Je ne crains rien si tu m'as reconnue.
Mon Amour, de bien loin, pour toi, je suis venue
Peut-être. Et nous irons Dieu sait où maintenant?
Depuis quand cherchais-tu mon ombre évanouie?
Quand t'avais-je perdu? Dans quelle vie?
Et qu'oserait le ciel contre nous maintenant?

The Path of Sand

Not to remember as we trod the sand...
Not to remember... I gave you my hand.
Our shadows' single tread
Blended as one, went trotting on ahead.
We looked off in the distance, or close by
Now and again. The air smelled then as I
Can smell it now. No Ocean wind... A dead
Calm, not a breeze from anywhere. The sky,
Cloudless. And there, a pine that, once upon
A time, was two, but that now stood alone,
Its twin chopped down. And on we walked, and on
We talked—or didn't—sure that we would own
That hour fair, hold it ever in our hands!...
Don't stop to look back when you walk the sands.

The Path of Love

Love, dearest Love, I know you're next to me,
So fair of face. You may
Change your name, age, your heart, the way
You speak... But your face cannot faithless be.
Those eyes that light your face, Love, next to me,
Shine, patient as the stars. If you but nod,
I fear no night, vast seas, bleak isles... For you,
I've come, Love, from afar, perhaps. Whereto
Do we go now, we two? Good God,
Who knows? How long have you been searching now
To find my shadow, vanished in thin air?
When did I lose you, Love? In what life? Where?
And how can heaven dare to undo us now?

Le Chemin de crève-cœur

Un seul cœur? Impossible
Si c'est par lui qu'on souffre et que l'on est heureux.
On dit: cœur douloureux,
Cœur torturé, cœur en lambeaux.
Puis: joyeux et léger comme un oiseau des Iles,
Un cœur si grand, si lourd, si gros
Qu'il n'y a plus de place
Pour rien d'autre que lui dans notre corps humain.
Puis évadé, baigné d'une grâce divine?
Un cœur si plein
De tout le sang du monde et ne gardant la trace
Que d'une cicatrice fine qui s'efface?
Impossible! Il me faut plusieurs cœurs.
Le même ne peut pas oublier dans la joie
Tout ce qu'il a connu de détresse une fois—
Une fois ou plusieurs, chaque fois pour toujours—
Et ne serait jamais un cœur neuf, sans patrie,
Sans bagage à porter de vie en vie.

Le Chemin de Dieu

Il est plusieurs chemins
dans le Royaume de mon père...
S'ils se côtoient,
se croisent ou s'ignorent,
ont leurs pentes de joie,
leurs gouffres, leurs clairières
et leur faune et leur flore,
n'importe. Il est plusieurs chemins.

The Heartbreak Path

One heart? Just one? Oh, that can't be,
If it gives us both joy and bitterness.
We speak about "a heart's distress",
"Heart, sore with pain and misery",
"A shattered, tattered heart..." But then, no less,
We say that it's light as a feather,
Gay as an Island bird! We can't choose whether
It's a huge, weighty load that leaves no space
Whatever for the body's other parts—
Only the heart's—
Or something free as air and bathed in grace?
Heart full of all the world's blood, with a trace
Of a thin scar that time erases?... No!
One heart? Just one? Oh, that can't be! And, though
Joys come and go, the joys of one alone
Cannot dispel the woe that it has known—
Once or forever! Nor can one heart be
Made new, or shun its endless destiny,
From life to life, free of what it has sown.

God's Path

Many the roads, the ways, to reach
my father's Kingdom, whether
they criss-cross or lie each by each,
known or unknown each to the rest, together...
Slopes of joy, or abysses, or a
cluster of clearings with their fauna, flora,
no matter. Many the roads, the ways.

Il est plusieurs montagnes
de hauteur différente
avec plusieurs versants...
et bien des taupinières
où grimpent des fourmis.
Si nul ne t'accompagne
que l'ombre de ton corps sur le cadran solaire,
mettras-tu plus de temps
à gravir la montagne?

Si tu dors sous la tente
des riches caravanes,
mettras-tu moins de temps
à sortir des savanes?

Si tu n'as pas d'amis
dont la barque et les rames
aient bravé la tempête aux quatre coins du monde,
mettras-tu plus de temps pour atteindre le port
que vous n'en auriez mis
ramant ensemble?
Quels chemins se ressemblent!

Tant de lames profondes
et de côtes sans fjords,
tant de vagues de sable
autour de minarets,
tant de neige et de vent
sur le mont Everest...

Et le chemin de Dieu peut être si modeste.

Many the summits tall that raise
their peaks to differing height
on many a rising face...
Many the mounds where ants creep, crawl apace.
And if you climb against the light,
alone—your shadow on the sundial cast—
then tell me, will more time have passed
before you reach the mountain's height?

Or, if you sleep beneath rich tents
in caravans of opulence,
then tell me, will less time have passed
before you quit life's flatland space?

Or if you have no friends whose skiff
defied the storm in earth's immensity,
then tell me, will more time have passed before
you reach the port, more time than if
you rowed together, oar to oar?
Oh, how alike those paths can be!

So many a current, swirling deep,
coasts' fjordless silhouettes,
so many the whirling sands that sweep
about tall minarets,
so many the Everest storms, the snow,
the gusts that blow...

And God's path, calm in its simplicity.

Le Chemin creux

Le vieux chemin creusé d'ornières?
Il a trop plu.
Le vieux chemin de la Carrière,
Celui du vieux moulin qui ne moud plus,
Le chemin du Seigneur qui n'a plus de château,
Le chemin du Bourreau,
Le chemin de la malle-poste,
Et ceux qui les croisaient, tous les chemins herbus,
Tous les chemins pleins d'eau,
Tous les chemins perdus...
Entre les ronces hautes,
Les prunelliers, la douce-amère, les bryones,
Le vert était celui des grottes et le jaune
Celui de la mélancolie.
Même le gel craquant sous le pas des brebis
Y devient triste avant la nuit tombée.
Les chemins creux, la pluie,
Le givre gris,
Le dernier scarabée...

Prenons la route neuve
Qui sur un pont solide et neuf passe le fleuve.

The Sunken Road

The old road, rutted deep? Ah yes,
It rained so much.
Time was, the old post road, I guess,
The road where Seigneur Such-and-such
Had his chateau, now un-chateaued,
The road where ground the ancient mill,
Grinding no more, silent and still.
Old Hangman's Road...
And all those roads, grass-covered paths, criss-crossed.
Roads lying hidden, lost...
And there, among the briars that rose
Up tall, the blackthorns and the brionies,
The bittersweets... Grotto greens, these,
And melancholic yellow, those.
And the freeze, crackling with lambs' soft footfall,
Grows sad even before the setting sun.
Sunken roads, rain, gray pall
Of frost over it all...
A beetle... The last one...

Let's take the new road, with its new
Stone bridge over the river, passing through...

Le Chemin des hauts-plateaux

I

C'est le chemin des hauts-plateaux,
Le petit chemin sec en bordure du ciel.
Un chêne rabougri s'y dresse entre les ronces.
Des vallons bleus s'enfoncent
Des deux côtés comme deux sillons d'eau
Contre un vaisseau de pierre.
Et l'herbe et la broussaille et la pierre et la terre
Sont craquantes et dures
Sur le pont du vaisseau qu'ont fui les matelots.
Sans hublots, sans mâture,
Le plateau se découpe en bordure du ciel.
Dans sa maigre verdure ou ses haillons de bure,
Le chêne y veille seul, debout, en proie au vent,
Au soleil, à la lune, à l'ombre, frissonnant
D'un frisson éternel.

II

Sur l'autre promontoire
Un bouquet d'arbres noirs
Fut le Bois des Supplices.
Quand dort l'oiseau de jour
L'oiseau de nuit s'y glisse
A rames de velours
En bordure du ciel...

Pujols, chemin de la Corniche.

The Road to the High Plateaus

I

It's the road to the High Plateaus,
Little dry road by heaven's edge lying.
Among the briars a stunted dwarf oak grows.
On either side, valley slopes, bluish, steep—
Like water slapping, in a twofold wake,
A ship of stone—plunge hard and deep.
The rocks, the grass, the brambles make
Harsh cracklings over the vast deck that, now,
The sailors have abandoned, fled.
No mast, no portholes on the vessel, spread
Its length from stern to bow
In silhouette, by heaven's edge lying.
Rag-clad in sickly green or burlap-browned,
The oak—alone, bold—holds its ground
Against the wind, sun, moon, night's darkening,
Never off-guard, and shuddering
A shudder chill, ever undying...

II

The other cliff has stood
Tree-blackened, like a Wood
Of Wrack and Woe. And when
The bird of day sleeps, then
The bird of night, with oars
Of softest velvet, soars
The space by heaven's edge lying...

Pujols, the road to the Corniche

Le Chemin des hors-la-loi

C'est le chemin des hors-la-loi
Sans pavés. Sans poteaux ni bornes.
Sans fils télégraphiques
En portées de musique.
Sans affiches rouges ou jaunes.
Sans rivière, sans pont du Roy,
Sans maisons, sans clochers, sans rien.
Un chemin sans troupeau ni chien
Sous une lune qui s'écorne
Toute seule au milieu du ciel.
Chemins, chemins habituels
Faits pour les gens en uniforme
Vous nous menez chacun sait où.
Mais la lune a des complaisances
Pour les rebelles et les fous.
Et quand l'aventure commence
Elle transpose on ne sait où
Le petit chemin sans ornières,
Sans bannières et sans frontières,
Qui peut-être un jour fut à nous.

The Outlaws' Way

Outlaws' Way... It's the road where knaves
And brigands used to come and go.
Rough and unpaved. No mileposts, no
Telegraph poles, no wires like staves
Of music strung between. No red
Or yellow highway signs outspread.
No streams, no King's bridge spanning one.
No houses, steeples, belfries... None,
Nothing. A simple road, just so.
No flocks, no dogs. Lying below
A wasting moon, aglow mid-sky.
Alone. Not like you, everyday
Roads... Roads where uniformed array
Lead us on, we know where and why.
Oh, but the moon contrives to do
What fools and rebels want her to,
And moves to who knows where or why
The rutless path—anonymous,
No frontier but the endless sky—
That once may have belonged to us.

Château de Biron

Sur les chemins nus, plus personne.
Couleur de sanguine pâlie
Un horizon de bois frissonne.
De quelle âpre mélancolie
Nous enveloppe ici l'automne?

Un gémissement de poulie
Survit seul en haut du puits rond.
La cour d'honneur et le perron
En vain parleraient d'Italie...
Trop de couloirs sombres relient
Aux salles où nos pas résonnent
Des retraits que nous ignorons.
Trop d'ombre se tasse aux chevrons
Le long de frises abolies.

Feu le duc aux "souliers tout ronds"
A rejoint défunt Bragelonne.
Dans les cuisines, plus personne.
Le soir meurt, plein de moucherons.
Vieux château des Gontaut-Biron
Avec quelle mélancolie
Vous regardez venir l'automne...

The Château de Biron

Empty the roads. Now, nobody...
Blood-orange hued, dimly out there,
Horizon trembling tree to tree...
What autumn melancholy, bare
And bleak, hugs us with sullen air?

A pulley's querulous melody—
Lone vestige—creaks atop the well.
The court, the castle-stair, would tell
In vain their tales of Italy...
So many dark halls leading on
To darkened alcoves, corners where
Our footsteps echo hollowly.
So dark the friezes, too, whereon
Molders an antique filigree.

Duke "of the round shoes", dead and gone,
Has joined the late Count Bragelonne.
Now, in the kitchens, no one, nobody.
Gnats swarm the dying dusk... And there,
Old Château de Biron, you see—
With melancholy, bleak and bare—
Autumn coming to fill the air...

La Grotte des lépreux

Vallée du Gavaudun

Ne me parlez ni de la tour,
Ni des belles ruines rousses,
Ni de cette vivante housse
De feuillages en demi-jour.

La gorge est trop fraîche et trop verte;
La rivière, comme un serpent,
S'y tord, à peine découverte
Sous trop d'herbe où reste en suspens
Le mystère des forêts vierges.

Ne me parlez ni de l'auberge,
Ni des écrevisses qu'on prend
Dans la mousse et les capillaires.

Je n'ai vu, de ce coin de terre,
Ni la paix du soir transparent,
Ni celle des crêtes désertes.

Mais, barrant le ciel, deux rochers
Tout à coup si nus, écorchés,
Avec plusieurs bouches ouvertes!

Vers ces bouches noires, clamant
On ne sait quelle horreur ancienne,
Savez-vous si, furtivement,
De pauvres âmes ne reviennent?

Où sont-ils, où sont-ils, mon Dieu,
Ces parias vêtus de rouge
Qui, là-haut, guettaient les soirs bleus
Par les trous béants de ce bouge?

The Lepers' Grotto

The Gavaudun Valley

Don't talk to me about its tower,
About its ruins reddening,
About its foliage blanketing
In shade the dim-lit leafy bower.

The gorge is all too cool, too green.
The stream goes trickling, snakes its course
Between the rocks, twists, scarcely seen—
Too thick the grass!—where forest gorse
Holds its breath's virgin mystery.

Don't talk about its inn to me,
About the river's moss and fern,
And crayfish caught at every turn.

Twilight's transparent peace was not
What I saw in this calm sojourn,
Nor the high crests that time forgot.

No. There against the sky I saw,
Suddenly, two cliffs—rocks spread bare,
Ragged—with many a yawning jaw.

To those black mouths, wailing with their
Who-knows-what age-old baleful yearning,
Don't ghosts come back? Aren't you aware
Of poor souls furtively returning?

Where are they? Where, my God, those souls,
Pariahs clad in red, and who,
Up there, peered at the skies of blue
Through that hell-haunt's wide-gaping holes?

Grotte des Lépreux, seuil maudit
Au bord de la falaise ocreuse...
Il faudrait qu'on ne m'eût pas dit
Quel frisson traversait jadis
Ce décor de feuilles heureuses...

Le Chemin des jardins

Jusqu'ici le cœur se cachait dans l'arbre
et l'arbre touffu savait le défendre.
Mais les émondeurs tourmentèrent l'arbre.
Le cœur s'en alla.

Dans le vieux jardin le lierre espéra.
Mais le nouveau maître en voulait au lierre
et tout ce qui grimpe et tout ce qui dure
fut déraciné.

Au bord du grenier les nids d'hirondelles
auraient pu cacher le cœur exilé
mais sous un toit neuf que peut la gênoise
dans sa nudité?

Ni toit ni jardin n'ont plus d'ombre sûre.
si même la sauge avait refleuri
rien ne cacherait la Vierge Marie.

Quand l'arbre n'eut plus que deux bras en croix
où le cœur s'en fut, on ne le sait pas.

The Lepers' Grotto!... Cursed threshold
Into the cliffs' ochre recesses...
How I wish I had not been told
What shudders racked, in days of old,
This realm of leafy lovelinesses...

The Gardens' Path

Till then the heart was hiding in the tree,
and the tree thick with leaves protected it.
But then the pruners came, tortured the tree.
And the heart fled.

In the old garden ivy's hope ran high.
But the new owner scorned it utterly,
and everything that clings and grows and lasts
was ripped out dead.

Beside the grain-filled lofts the swallows' nests
might well have kept the exiled heart concealed.
But what good is a naked eave beneath
a fine new roof?

Now neither roof's nor garden's shade is sure.
And if the sage had blossomed yet once more,
even the Virgin could not hide within.

Now the tree stood, cross-like, in two-armed pose.
Where did the heart go fleeing? No one knows.

ILLNESS

Vous parler?

Vous parler? Non. Je ne peux pas.
Je préfère souffrir comme une plante,
Comme l'oiseau qui ne dit rien sur le tilleul.
Ils attendent. C'est bien. Puisqu'ils ne sont pas las
D'attendre, j'attendrai, de cette même attente.

Ils souffrent seuls. On doit apprendre à souffrir seul.
Je ne veux pas d'indifférents prêts à sourire
Ni d'amis gémissants. Que nul ne vienne.

La plante ne dit rien. L'oiseau se tait. Que dire?
Cette douleur est seule au monde, quoi qu'on veuille.
Elle n'est pas celle des autres, c'est la mienne.

Une feuille a son mal qu'ignore l'autre feuille,
Et le mal de l'oiseau, l'autre oiseau n'en sait rien.

On ne sait pas. On ne sait pas. Qui se ressemble?
Et se ressemblât-on, qu'importe. Il me convient
De n'entendre ce soir nulle parole vaine.

J'attends—comme le font derrière la fenêtre
Le vieil arbre sans geste et le pinson muet...
Une goutte d'eau pure, un peu de vent, qui sait?
Qu'attendent-ils? Nous l'attendrons ensemble.
Le soleil leur a dit qu'il reviendrait, peut-être...

To Speak, to Tell You?

To speak, to tell you? No, I can't.
I'd rather bear my suffering like a bird—
Perched silent in the linden tree, unheard—
Or even waiting, like a patient plant...
Waiting... Yes, like them I wait patiently.

Alone, they suffer. We must learn to bear
Our pain alone. Let no friend come bestow
A hypocritic smile or moan on me.

Mute is the plant; the bird, still. What is there
For them to say? Like it or not, this woe
Of mine is all my own. No others share it.

One leaf's distress, one bird's, will always be
Unknown to others. Bird and leaf must bear it.

Unknown... Unknown... Are others like us? No.
And, if they were, what would it matter? Here,
Tonight, I have no wish to listen to
A lot of chatter... So, let time elapse...

Mute as the finch, still as the old tree near
My window, I wait... For a drop of dew?
A breeze? Who knows? We'll wait together though.
The sun promised them to return, perhaps...

Médecins

Ne cherchez donc pas dans vos livres!
Est-il si compliqué de vivre?
Quel mal ils m'auront fait, ces tristes médecins...
Je ne dis pas que ce soit à dessein
Et l'on n'est pas toujours exprès des assassins;
Mais tant de drogues, de piqûres,
Et si peu de savoir? Ils me tueront, c'est clair.

Me laisser tant souffrir, souffrir tout un hiver,
Pour jouer ensuite aux Augures!

Je les vois en bouchers me palper tour à tour,
Puis s'enfermer d'un air sinistre—
Conseil de guerre? de ministres?
Concile? Ou, verrous clos, sous l'abat-jour,
La conspiration de mélo, dans la cave?
Je rirais bien, si ce n'était beaucoup plus grave.
Mais il s'agit de moi qui ne sais rien
Et de ces gens à qui, dirait-on, j'appartiens,
Parce qu'ils font semblant de savoir quelque chose.

Bouchut en sait mille fois plus, hélas!
Mon vieux Bouchut qui prend son herbe et se la dose
Et toujours se guérit des misères qu'il a
Sans en chercher la cause...

Vieux Bouchut, vieux Bouchut, dans ton bain de soleil,
Tu te moques de leurs remèdes!
Ton ventre est chaud, ton petit nez vermeil.
Tu me suffis, Bouchut. Viens à mon aide...

Doctors

Don't look for answers in your books!
Is living as hard as it looks?
What harm these sad-faced doctors will have done me!
It's not on purpose that they'll run me
Into the ground. If only they would shun me
With all their medicines, and drugs, and shots.
And yet, so little knowledge! Killers kill
Sometimes by chance. With me, that's how they will...

To let me suffer, only to draw lots
After a wintertime of suffering!

I see them, one by one, examining
And poking me, like butchers, then
Hiding away to frown and fret—
Council of war? The cabinet?
Conspiracy? Or, then again,
Some somber melodrama played by night
Behind locked doors in cellar's shadowed light?
I'd laugh if it weren't serious! But when
I realize it's me, that I belong
To them, and that they're wrong... All of them, wrong...

My old Bouchut's a thousand times more clever,
Taking his dose of catnip for whatever
Comes along, pains him, ails him, goes awry,
And never knowing how or why...

Bouchut, Bouchut, old friend! Lazing out in the sun...
You meow your scorn for all their remedies!
Warm belly, pink snout... Little one,
You're all I need, Bouchut. Come, help me please...

Un Médecin?

Un médecin? Mais alors qu'il soit beau!
Très beau. D'une beauté non pas majestueuse,
Mais jeune, saine, alerte, heureuse!
Qu'il parle de plein air, non pas trop haut,
Mais assez pour que du soleil entre avec lui.

Qu'il sache rire—tant d'ennui
Bâille aux quatre coins de la chambre—
Et qu'il sache te faire rire, toi, souffrant
De ta souffrance et du mal de Décembre.

Décembre gris, Décembre gris, Noël errant
Sous un ciel de plomb et de cendre.
Un médecin doit bien savoir
D'où ce gris mortel peut descendre?

Qu'il soit gai pour vaincre le soir
Et les fantômes de la fièvre.
Qu'il dise les mots qu'on attend
Ou qu'on les devine à ses lèvres.

Qu'il soit gai, qu'il soit bien portant
(Ne faut-il croire à l'équilibre
Qui doit redevenir le nôtre, aux membres libres,
A l'esprit jouant sans efforts?)
Qu'il soit bien portant, qu'il soit fort—sans insolence,
Avec douceur, contre le sort...
Il nous faut tant de confiance!

Qu'il aime ce que j'aime—j'ai besoin
Qu'il ait cet art de tout comprendre
Et de s'intéresser, non pas de loin,
Mais en ami tout proche, à ce qui m'intéresse.

A Doctor?

A doctor? Well, at least let him be fair,
Good-looking! But not all haughtily so.
Healthy, young, spirits high... Voice low—
To talk about the out-of-doors, fresh air—
Just loud enough to bring some sunlight in.

Let him know how to laugh—chagrin
Yawns in the corners of this sickroom, fills
It full—and how to make you laugh, poor thing,
Sick with your sickness and December ills.

December! Gray!... Christmas, meandering
Beneath a lead-and-ashen sky...
All of that dead December gray, descending...
Oughtn't a doctor know the "whence," the "why"?

Let him be bright and gay at daylight's ending,
Rout fever's ghosts and night's unrest.
Let him tell us what we would like to hear:
Comforting words, spoken aloud or guessed.

Let him be bright and gay, full of good cheer.
Give him good health. (Oughtn't he make us see
A picture of the vigor that will be
Our own when, free of mind and cured of limb,
We will be strong and healthy too, like him?)
Give him good health and strength, defense
Against fate's blows, but gentle, not
Arrogant toward our woes and human lot...
Oh how we need to feel his confidence!

Let him like what I like: I must
Know that he has that art of comprehending
All my concerns, but as a friend I trust,
Not just some distant somebody, pretending.

Qu'il soit bon—nous voulons une indulgence tendre
Pour accepter notre révolte ou nos faiblesses.

De la science? Il en aura, n'en doutez point,
S'il est ce que je dis, ce que j'exige.

Mais exiger cela, c'est, vous le voyez bien,
Leur demander, quand ils n'y peuvent rien,
Quelque chose comme un prodige!

Lequel, parmi vos diplômés,
Ressemble au médecin qu'espère le malade?
Lequel, dans tout ce gris tenace, épais, maussade,
Sera celui que moi je vois, les yeux fermés?...

                    • • •

Ou bien, alors, prenons-le contrefait,
Cagneux, pointu, perclus, minable;
Qu'il flotte en ses effets
Comme un épouvantail—et semble inguérissable
Des pires maux, connus ou inconnus!

Prenons-le blême et vieux, que son crâne soit nu,
Ses yeux rougis, sa lèvre amère—
Et que rien ne paraisse au monde plus précaire,
Plus laid, plus rechigné que cet être vivant,

Afin que, chaque jour, l'apercevant
Comme un défi, parmi les fleurs venant d'éclore,
Nous pensions, rassurés, soulagés, fiers un peu
De nous sentir si forts par contraste: "Grand Dieu!
Qu'il doit être savant pour vivre encore!"

Let him be kind and good, indulgent for
The feelings of revolt our weakness breeds.

Knowledge? Science? Of course! To suit my needs,
He must have oh so much, and even more!

But fruitless are the cures at their command!
I fear that my demands would take
At least a miracle for my poor sake!

And so, in all this deep, gray devastation,
In all your doctor-titled band,
Is there one like the one I hope for, and
The one I see in my imagination?

• • •

If not, let's have one squat, unfit—
One who, knock-kneed and crippled, nasty, vile,
Clings to his clothing, swims in it,
Scarecrow-like, and who suffers all the while
From all the fatal ills known and unknown.

Let's have one old, bald, pale, down to the bone,
Eyes rimmed with red, lips wizened, cold—
Such that no one could be, if truth be told,
Uglier or more nearly dead than he—

So that, each day, on his arrival, we
See him—midst flowers fresh-blooming on the sill—
Defy death!, and think, with a sigh, somewhat
Proud to look well compared to him: "God! But
What skill he must have, to be living still!"

Jours de fièvre

Ce que je veux? Une carafe d'eau glacée.
Rien de plus. Nuit et jour, cette eau, dans ma pensée,
Ruisselle doucement comme d'une fontaine.
Elle est blanche, elle est bleue à force d'être fraîche.
Elle vient de la source ou d'une cruche pleine.
Elle a cet argent flou qui duvète les pêches
Et l'étincellement d'un cristal à facettes.

Elle est de givre fin, de brouillard, de rosée,
Jaillit de chaque vasque en gerbes irisées,
Glisse de chaque branche en rondes gouttelettes.
Au coeur de la carafe, elle rit. Elle perle
Sur son ventre poli, comme une sueur gaie.
En mille petits flots, pour rien, elle déferle,
Ou n'est qu'un point comme un brillant dans une haie.

Elle danse au plafond, se complaît dans la glace,
Frappe aux carreaux avec la pluie. Ah! ces cascades...
C'est le Niagara, vert bleu, vert Nil, vert jade,
C'est l'eau miraculeuse en un fleuve de grâce;
Toute l'eau des névés, des lacs, des mers nordiques,
Toute l'eau du Rocher de Moïse, l'eau pure
D'une oasis perdue au centre de l'Afrique;

Toute l'eau qui mugit, toute l'eau qui murmure,
Toute l'eau, toute l'eau du ciel et de la terre,
Toute l'eau concentrée au creux glacé d'un verre!
Je ne demande rien qu'un verre d'eau glacée...

Fever Days

What do I want? Only a pitcher, chilled,
With ice-cold water. Day and night, my dreaming,
Yearning, desiring... All my thoughts are filled
With that fresh and cool, blue-white water, streaming
Endless, as from a brimming jug, a spring,
Silvered, like peaches' downy covering,
Or crystal, gleaming, many-faceted.

A dew, a gentle mist, a frosty haze
Spurt from each bowl in opaline bouquets
And drip from every branch with droplets spread.
There, in the pitcher's breast, it gleefully
Laughs, and it beads up in a merry sweat
That shines its belly, or flows in a spree,
Unfurled, or sparkles like a gem, hedge-set.

It dances on the ceiling; it inspects
With pride its image as the glass reflects
The rain, striking each window-pane... Cascades...
Niagara's blue-greens, the Nile's deep green jades...
Water... A miracle of liquid grace!
Lakes, glacial snows, and northland seas. And Moses'
Rock! Pure oasis African, that dozes
Hidden... Waters of every time and place!

Waters that weep, waters that roar!
Waters... Waters of earth, waters of sky...
Waters... All in the space of one chilled glass!
Ice water, just one glass! I ask no more...

Vous ne voyez donc pas mes doigts brûlants de fièvre,
Mes doigts tendus vers l'eau qui fuit? Mes pauvres lèvres
Sèches comme une plante à la tige cassée?
La soif qui me torture est celle des grands sables
Où galope toujours le simoun. Je ne pense
Qu'à ce filet d'eau merveilleuse, intarissable,
Où des poissons heureux circulent. Transparence,
Fraîcheur... Est-il rien d'autre au monde que j'implore?

Alcarazas, alcarazas... Un café maure
Et, dans la torpeur bleue où des buveurs s'attardent,
Un verre débordant parmi les autres verres,
Un verre sans couleurs subtiles qui le fardent,
Mais rempli de cette eau si froide, nette, claire...
Ah! prenez pour cette eau ce qui me reste à vivre,
Mais laissez-la couler en moi, larmes de givre,
Don de l'hiver à ce brasier qui me consume.

Vous souvient-il de ces bruits clairs, dans de l'écume,
Au bord d'un gave fou? J'ai soif de tous les gaves.
Les sabots des mulets, vous souvient-il, s'y lavent,
Les pieds du chemineau s'y délassent. Dieu juste,
Ne puis-je boire au moins comme le pré, l'arbuste,
Le chien de la montagne au fil de l'eau qui court?
Cette eau... Cette eau qui m'échappe toujours,
Qui, nuit et jour, obsède ma pensée...
Ne m'accorderez-vous deux gouttes d'eau glacée?

What? Can't you see my feverish fingers yearning,
Reaching out, and the glass, retreating, spurning
My grasp? My poor lips, burning, like a dry,
Withered stem, bent in two? Thirst tortures me
Like a simoun that gallops stormily,
Beating the arid desert sands. And I,
Tormented, dream of fish, cavorting free
In a cool, limpid brook... Water! What more
Is there for me to long for, languish for?

Alcarazas, alcarazas... Café
In whose dank, blue-gray Moorish atmosphere,
Where loll and linger its *habitués*,
A glass stands tall. Glass, colorless and clear,
Filled with ice water!... Ah! How I would give,
Gladly, the life I might yet have to live
If winter's gift—those tears of frost—might pour
Into me, quench each life-consuming ember!

Those bright sounds in the froth... Do you remember
How clear they were beside the torrent's shore,
Foaming along its course? I thirst for all
Those torrents wild, where mules—do you recall?—
Come bathe their hooves, and travelers laze. Good God!
Can't I, at least, drink like the bush, the sod,
The field, the dog who laps that mountain stream?
Cold water... Water that must ever seem
To flee my endless longing, days, nights through...
What? Won't you let me sip a drop or two?

Douleur, je vous déteste

L'Honneur de souffrir
Anna de Noailles

Douleur, je vous déteste! Ah! que je vous déteste!
Souffrance, je vous hais, je vous crains, j'ai l'horreur
De votre guet sournois, de ce frisson qui reste
Derrière vous, dans la chair, dans le coeur...

Derrière vous, parfois vous précédant,
J'ai senti cette chose inexprimable, affreuse:
Une bête invisible aux minuscules dents
Qui vient comme la taupe et fouille et mord et creuse
Dans la belle santé confiante—pendant
Que l'air est bleu, le soleil calme, l'eau si fraîche!

Ah! "l'Honneur de souffrir"?... Souffrance aux lèvres sèches,
Souffrance laide, quoi qu'on dise, quel que soit
Votre déguisement... Souffrance
Foudroyante ou tenace ou les deux à la fois,
Moi je vous vois comme un péché, comme une offense
A l'allègre douceur de vivre, d'être sain
Parmi des fruits luisants, des feuilles vertes,
Des jardins faisant signe aux fenêtres ouvertes...

De gais canards courent vers les bassins,
Des pigeons nagent sur la ville, fous d'espace.
Nager, courir, lutter avec le vent qui passe,
N'est-ce donc pas mon droit puisque la vie est là
Si simple en apparence... en apparence!

Faut-il être ces corps vaincus, ces esprits las,
Parce qu'on vous rencontre un jour, Souffrance,
Ou croire à cet honneur de vous appartenir
Et dire qu'il est grand, peut-être, de souffrir?

Pain, I Abhor You

Honor in suffering
Anna de Noailles

Pain, I abhor you! Oh! How sly I find you!
Suffering, how I loathe your stealthy art:
Spying, lying in wait, leaving behind you
That shuddering through my body, soul, and heart...

Behind you, and at times even before you,
I've felt that nameless, fearsome thing, so keen,
So sharp! O, how I dread you more and more, you
Tiny-toothed, biting beast, clawing unseen,
Like a mole, gnawing at the flesh,
Brimming with health, while blue the air
And calm the sun, the waters cool and fresh!

"Honor in suffering"? What honor? Where?
O ugly, parch-lipped Suffering!
Say what you will, whatever be your guise,
Whether swift lightning blow or lingering
Your ill—or both—no matter. In my eyes
You sin against life's sprightly cheer, against
Its bright-skinned fruits, new leaves, life scarce commenced,
Gardens beyond our window's beckoning...

Ducks waddle gaily toward the ponds, unfenced,
And pigeons, drunk on space, swim on the breeze.
Run, swim, battle roof-skimming winds... Should these
Simple delights not be my right as well?
The joy of living, it would seem... would seem...

Must I be one of those who can but dream
Of robust flesh and wit, because some tell
How fine it is to pay you fealty,
And what great honor suffering can be!

Grand? Qui donc en est sûr et que m'importe!
Que m'importe le nom du mal, grand ou petit,
Si je n'ai plus en moi, candide et forte,
La Joie au clair visage? Il s'est menti,
Il se ment à lui-même, le poète
Qui, pour vous ennoblir, vous chante... Je vous hais.

Vous êtes lâche, injuste, criminelle, prête
Aux pires trahisons! Je sais
Que vous serez mon ennemie infatigable
Désormais... Désormais, puisqu'il ne se peut pas
Que le plus tendre parc embaumé de lilas,
Le plus secret chemin d'herbe folle ou de sable,
Permettent de vous fuir ou de vous oublier!

Chère ignorance en petit tablier,
Ignorance aux pieds nus, aux bras nus, tête nue
A travers les saisons, ignorance ingénue
Dont le rire tintait si haut. Mon Ignorance,
Celle d'Avant, quand vous m'étiez une inconnue,
Qu'en a-t-on fait, qu'en faites-vous, vieille Souffrance?

Vous pardonner cela qui me change le monde?
Je vous hais trop! Je vous hais trop d'avoir tué
Cette petite fille blonde
Que je vois comme au fond d'un miroir embué...
Une Autre est là, pâle, si différente!

Je ne peux pas, je ne veux pas m'habituer
A vous savoir entre nous deux, toujours présente,
Sinistre Carabosse à qui les jeunes fées
Opposent vainement des Pouvoirs secourables!

Il était une fois...
Il était une fois—pauvres voix étouffées!
Qui les ranimera, qui me rendra la voix
De cette Source, fée entre toutes les fées,
Où tous les maux sont guérissables?

Great? Says who? Should I care? Should I
Care what they call the curse, what name they give—
Long one or short?—if it won't let me live
With simple, rugged, fair-faced joy! Oh, why,
Why does the poet sing your praises, try
To make you noble? Lies! Lies!... I detest you!

Cowardly, craven, traitor plague-possessed, you
Shrink before no excess! I know you will
Be tireless in your endless enmity,
From now on... From now on, so foul the ill
That no lush lilac, wafting fragrantly,
No hidden, sand-strewn path, wild grasses' scents,
Let me forget or flee your virulence!

Dear Ignorance naïve, pert, apron-dressed—
Year after year, gentle insouciance...
Bare arms, bare feet, head bare—my Ignorance,
Whose laughter rang out clear, Ignorance blessed,
From my Before, when you were still unknown...
What have you done with it, O Suffering?

Forgive you, with my world so wasted grown
Because of you? Ah no! No pardoning!
I hate you! Hate you so for killing her—
Blond child, a mirror's misty blur...
An Other takes her place, pallid and wan!

Never can I, never will I defer
To you, vile, wretched Hag, witch woebegone,
Who lurk betwixt me and my disarray:
Good fairies work their powers in vain thereon!

In bygone day...
In bygone day... Poor voices, stifled, stilled!
Who will revive their promise, unfulfilled—
The fairy Source that lovingly assured
That there was no pain that could not be cured?

Ah! Laissez-moi crier

Ah! laissez-moi crier, crier, crier...
Crier à m'arracher la gorge!
Crier comme une bête qu'on égorge,
Comme le fer martyrisé dans une forge,
Comme l'arbre mordu par les dents de la scie,
Comme un carreau sous le ciseau du vitrier...
Grincer, hurler, râler! Peu me soucie
Que des gens s'en effarent. J'ai besoin
De crier jusqu'au bout de ce qu'on peut crier.

Les gens? Vous ne savez donc pas comme ils sont loin,
Comme ils existent peu, lorsque vous supplicie
Cette douleur qui vous fait seul au monde?
Avec elle on est seul, seul dans sa geôle.
Répondre? Non. Je n'attends pas qu'on me réponde.
Je ne sais même pas si j'appelle au secours,
Si même j'ai crié, crié comme une folle,
Comme un damné, toute la nuit et tout le jour.
Cette chose inouïe, atroce, qui vous tue,
Croyez-vous qu'elle soit
Une chose possible à quoi l'on s'habitue?
Cette douleur, mon Dieu, cette douleur qui tue...
Avec quel art cruel de supplice chinois
Elle montait, montait, à petits pas sournois,
Et nul ne la voyait monter, pas même toi,
Confiante santé, ma santé méconnue!
C'est vers toi que je crie, ah! c'est vers toi, vers toi!
Pourquoi, si tu m'entends, n'être pas revenue?
Pourquoi me laisser tant souffrir, dis-moi pourquoi
Ou si c'est ta revanche et parce qu'autrefois
Jamais, simple santé, je ne pensais à toi.

Ah! Let me scream

Ah! Let me scream, scream, scream.... Let me
Scream till my throat bursts, scream my agony,
Like a beast when its throat is being slit,
Like red hot iron when blacksmith hammers it,
Scream like the martyred, harried tree
Ripped by the saw's teeth, like the window-pane
Beneath the glazier's chisel... Scream, again,
Again... Shriek, screech... So what if my
Screaming upsets and frightens people? I
Have to scream to the scream's farthermost reach!

People? Ah! You have no idea how far
Others can be when torment racks you! Each
And every one! Here, in this world, you are
Alone, imprisoned in your suffering.
Reply? No need. Do I expect
You to, or hope you can do anything
To help? No. I can't even recollect
If that was me, that creature who
Shrieked like a soul condemned the whole night through,
And all day long, like one gone mad! This vile
Pain, never known before, that eats at you,
Kills you... Do you suppose that, in a while,
You learn to bear it? Dear God! If you knew
How it came creeping, creeping, stealthily,
Sly as some vicious Chinese torture, through
And through... And no one saw, not even you,
Smug health of mine, my turncoat enemy!
It's you I scream to! Oh! It's you, it's you!
If you can hear, how can you bear to be
Unmoved? Not to come back? Oh, why? Why do
You let me anguish so? Or is it true
That you take your revenge, good health, to make me see
How wrong I was never to think of you?

Aux médecins qui viennent me voir

Je ne peux plus, je ne peux plus, vous voyez bien...
C'est tout ce que je puis.
Et vous me regardez et vous ne faites rien.
Vous dites que je peux, vous dites-aujourd'hui
Comme il y a des jours et des jours--que l'on doit
Lutter quand même et vous ne savez pas
Que j'ai donné toute ma pauvre force, moi,
Tout mon pauvre courage et que j'ai dans les bras
Tous mes efforts cassés, tous mes espoirs trompés,
Qui pèsent tant--si vous saviez!

Pourquoi ne pas comprendre? Au bois des Oliviers
Jésus de Nazareth pleurait, enveloppé
D'une moins lourde nuit que celle où je descends.
Il fait noir. Tout est laid, misérable, écoeurant,
Sinistre... Vainement, vous tentez en passant
Un absurde sourire auquel nul ne se prend.
C'est d'un geste raté, d'une voix sonnant faux
Que vous me promettez un secours pour demain.
Demain! C'est à présent, tout de suite, qu'il faut
Une main secourable dans ma main.

For the Doctors Who Come to See Me

Worn out, worn out... There's no more I can do.
You see my suffering,
You look at me, examine me, but you
Are powerless. You don't do anything.
And yet you keep on telling me... Today
(Like all the other days gone by!), you say
We can, we must try, try with all our might...
But if you only knew how much I've tried,
Struggled, until there is no strength, no fight
Left in my weary limbs. All hopes have died,
They weigh me down... If you could know!

Why don't you understand? When Jesus stood
Weeping, the dark night of the Olive wood
Weighed less on him than weighs on me my woe.
How black it is. How wretched is the whole
Of life—ugly and base—yet, as you stroll
Past, how you try to fool me and cajole
Me with a smile that wouldn't fool a soul.
An empty nod, a promise oh so fine,
But false! A cure tomorrow!... No! Now! Now!
I can't wait... I need someone now, somehow,
To lay a helping hand in mine.

Je suis à bout...
C'est tout ce que je peux souffrir, c'est tout.
Je ne peux plus, je ne crois plus, n'espère plus.
Vous n'avez pas voulu,
Pas su comprendre, et sans pitié
Vous me laissez mourir de ma souffrance... Au moins,
Faites-moi donc mourir comme on est foudroyé,
D'un seul coup de couteau, d'un coup de poing—
Ou d'un de ces poisons de fakir, vert et or,
Qui vous endorment pour toujours, comme on s'endort
Quand on a tant souffert, tant souffert jour et nuit
Que rien ne compte plus que l'oubli, rien que lui...

Maladie

Filliou... Je veux Filliou. Ne t'en va pas, Filliou.
Ferme la porte.
Sortir? Pour aller où?
Dis? Je ne veux pas que tu sortes!

J'ai tout le temps besoin de toi. Pour tout,
Pour t'avoir là. Reste, Filliou...

Si tu t'en vas, je sonnerai si fort, si fort,
Que les murailles tomberont toutes ensemble.

I'm finished, done...
I've suffered all I can, I can't go on.
Nothing left to believe, to hope for... No,
None of you know... You couldn't... None
Know what it's like for me to suffer so!
At least show me some pity. Let me die
Quick as a thunderbolt slashing the sky,
Or stabbed, or with a single mortal blow,
Or with some gold-green potion that a clever
Fakir concocts to make you sleep forever:
Pained, anguished sleep—night, day—so pain-beset
That all I yearn for now is to forget...

Illness

Filliou... I want Filliou... Don't go, Filliou!
Please, close the door.
Stay here, I want you to...
Where would you go? I beg of you...

I need you here with me. I need you more
And more each day. Don't go, Filliou...

Or else I'll ring my bell so loud... You'll see,
The walls will tremble, crumble suddenly.

Ma cloche vient de Chamonix. Elle ressemble
A celle qui chantait, l'été dernier, au bord
De ce vallon près de Ciboure. Tout le port
Y scintillait, tu te souviens? Tout le décor
S'assombrissait vers les montagnes—et la cloche
Montait dans le chemin tout proche.
Au cou d'une petite vache rousse
Elle a chanté peut-être aussi
Ma clarine à moi, celle-ci...

Filliou, Filliou, c'est à grandes secousses
Qu'elle se fâche, tu sais bien,
Si tu descends! Reviens...

Lis quelque chose, dis,
Quelque chose de gai... dis, tu n'as rien
De très comique, d'inédit?

Alors, assieds-toi là... Raconte-moi, Filliou,
Raconte...
On ne l'avait jamais fini, ce conte
Qui nous passionnait! Dis-le-moi jusqu'au bout...
C'est "Coeur de Nénuphar et Tige de Bambou",
Tu te souviens? Le soir, tu l'inventais pour nous
Et c'était merveilleux, si merveilleux, Filliou!
Raconte...

(inachevé)

My bell, from Chamonix... Just like the one
That sang, last summer, at Ciboure. The sun
Shimmered the port, the valley too. But when
The shadows gathered toward the mountains, then—
Remember?—up the path close by it went
Clanging... And mine, perhaps, as well...
This one, singing in its ascent,
Hanging about a chestnut calf... My bell...

Filliou, Filliou... You know how it
Will fly into a rage and have a fit
Each time you leave! Come, come...

Read me a story. Something gay,
To make me laugh. You must know some—
Old ones or new. What do you say?

Sit there and tell me one... Begin, Filliou.
Begin...
The one you left undone, that drew us in
So utterly! I want to hear it through.
You know, "Lotus's Heart, Stalk of Bamboo"...
You made it up one evening as we two
Listened, enthralled. Enthralled, Filliou!
Begin...

(unfinished)

Printemps

Et puis, c'est oublié.
Ai-je pensé, vraiment, ces choses-là?
Bon soleil, te voilà
Sur les bourgeons poisseux qui vont se déplier.

Le miracle est partout.
Le miracle est en moi qui ne me souviens plus.
Il fait clair, il fait gai sur les bourgeons velus;
Il fait beau—voilà tout.

Je m'étire, j'étends mes bras au bon soleil
Pour qu'il les dore comme avant, qu'ils soient pareils
Aux premiers abricots dans les feuilles de juin.

L'herbe ondule au fil du chemin
Sous le galop du vent qui rit.
Les pâquerettes ont fleuri.

Je viens, je viens! Mes pieds dansent tout seuls
Comme les pieds du vent rieur,
Comme ceux des moineaux sur les doigts du tilleul.

(Tant de gris au-dehors, de gris intérieur,
De pluie et de brouillard, était-ce donc hier?)

Ne me rappelez rien. Le ciel est si léger!
Vous ne saurez jamais tout le bonheur que j'ai
A sentir la fraîcheur légère de cet air.

Un rameau vert aux dents comme le "Passeur d'eau",
J'ai sans doute ramé bien des nuits, bien des jours...
Ne me rappelez rien. C'est oublié. Je cours
Sur le rivage neuf où pointent les roseaux.

Spring

And then, forgotten, done...
Am I really the one who thought such things?
There you are, dear, dear, sun,
Playing on sticky buds and blossomings.

Miracle, all about.
Miracle, that I can forget... Ah! See
How bright! How gay each sprout, all velvety!
How pleasant it is out...

I stretch my arms and let the sun beat down
To turn them, as before, a golden brown,
Like June's first leaf-enveloped apricots.

Grass sways in waves along the lane
As the wind, laughing, gallops, trots...
Daisies have bloomed to life again.

I'm coming! Like the sparrows' feet that prance
Over the linden-fingered tree,
Mine, like the laughing wind's, begin to dance...

(Inside and out, what somber grays were these!
Fog, rain... Just yesterday's? How can that be?)

No! Don't remind me... See how airily
Light the sky hangs! You'll never know how much
I revel in its cool and gentle touch.

Boatman-like, green twig in my teeth, I know
I must have rowed for days, nights... Don't remind me,
Now that I tread a shore where new reeds grow.
The past is all forgotten, all behind me...

Rameau vert du Passeur ou branche qu'apporta
La colombe de l'Arche, ah! la verte saveur
Du buisson que tondra la chèvre aux yeux rêveurs!

Etre chèvre sans corde, éblouie à ce tas
De bourgeons lumineux qui mettent un halo
Sur la campagne verte; aller droit devant soi
Dans le bruit de grelots
Du ruisseau vagabond; suivre n'importe quoi,
Sauter absurdement, pour sauter; rire au vent
Pour l'unique raison de rire... Comme Avant!

C'est l'oubli, je vous dis, l'oubli miraculeux.

Votre visage même à qui j'en ai voulu
De trop guetter le mien, je ne m'en souviens plus,
C'est un autre visage; et mes deux chats frileux,
Mon grand Dickette-chien sont d'autres compagnons
Faits pour gens bien portants, nouveaux, ressuscités.

Bon soleil, bon soleil, voici que nous baignons
Dans cette clarté chaude où va blondir l'été.

Hier n'existe plus. Qui donc parlait d'hier?
Il fait doux, il fait gai sur les bourgeons ouverts...

The Boatman's green twig, or that branch the dove
Brought to the Ark... Ah! The green savor of
That bush the dream-eyed goat will browse, strip bare!

To be a goat unfettered, gazing there
In startled awe at all that budding light
That haloes green the land, to follow right
Where leads the stream's tinkling meandering,
Leaping with mindless pleasure, gamboling
To, fro, and laughing, laughing at the breeze
Just for the joy of laughing, nothing more—
Leaping with joy, and laughing... Like Before.

A miracle, I said! No memories...

Your face... That very face I would abhor,
That spied on mine too much. Forgotten now!
But other faces... My two cats, who get
So shivery cold! And my big dog Dickette...
Companions, all of them, transformed somehow
To pets for healthy folk, now new a-borning!

O sun, dear sun! We bask in your clear rays
And in your blond-hued locks, summer adorning.

The past is gone. Who spoke of yesterdays?
Today!... Ah, what a fair and joyful morning!

Demain

Tout voir—je vous ai dit que je voulais tout voir,
Tout voir et tout connaître!
Ah! ne pas seulement le rêver... le pouvoir!
Ne pas se contenter d'une seule fenêtre
Sur un même horizon,
Mais dans chaque pays avoir une maison
Et flâner à son gré de l'une à l'autre—ou mieux,
Avoir cette maison roulante,
Cette maison volante, d'où les yeux
Peuvent aller plus loin, plus loin toujours! Attente
D'on ne sait quoi... je veux savoir ce qu'on attend.

Tout savoir... Tout savoir de l'univers profond,
Des êtres et des choses,
De la terre et des astres, jusqu'au fond.
Savoir la cause
De cet amour qu'on a pour des noms de pays,
Des noms qui chantent à l'oreille avec instance
Comme s'ils appelaient depuis longtemps,
Depuis toujours—des noms immenses
Dont on est envahi,
Ou des noms tout petits, presque ignorés.

Longs pays blancs du Nord, pays dorés
Du Sud ou du Levant plein de mystère....
Et les jeunes, aux villes claires:
New-York, San Francisco, Miami, des lumières,
Du bruit, de la vitesse, de l'espace...

Ah! tout voir, tout savoir des minutes qui passent,
De celles qui viendront...
Demain, comme je t'aime!

Tomorrow

To see it all, I said... To see and know
Everything... Not enough to dream, but be
Able to do it all! Not patiently
To sit beside a single window, see
The same horizon... No!
To have a house in every country, go
Lazing betwixt, between... Or, better still,
To have a house with wheels, with wings,
And let my eyes go gazing over things
Farther and farther off... To wait my fill—
For what? Who knows? I wish I knew.

To know it all... Yes, everything, throughout
The universe. To know the who,
The what... Earth, stars... Within, without...
Even know why
We love the music of those names that haunt us—
Vast country names that sing, forever taunt us,
Invade and occupy
Our mind, again, again... Or others, small,
And that we barely know at all.

Northern lands, stretching long and white,
Golden climes of the South, the mystery
Of the Levant, young ones with cities bright:
New York, Miami, San Francisco... Light,
And noise, and speed, spreading out endlessly...

To see it, know it all... Minutes gone by,
Minutes to come...
Tomorrow, how I love you!

Je ne fais qu'entr'ouvrir les yeux, lever le front,
Commencer de comprendre.
Hier, savais-je même
Ce que c'était que respirer dans le jour tendre?

Bonheur de voir, d'entendre,
Qui vient à vous dans un frisson;
Tant de beauté, tant de couleurs, de sons...
Royaume de la vie!

(inachevé)

I open my eyes and raise my brow...
Scarcely can I begin to try
To understand. Did I know yesterday
What breathing deep day's gentle breath could do?

To see, to hear... What joy! Array
Of beauty, colors, sounds that come to you
In a great shudder, through and through...
O you, kingdom of life!

(unfinished)

Quand je serai guérie

Filliou, quand je serai guérie,
Je ne veux voir que des choses très belles...

De somptueuses fleurs, toujours fleuries;
Des paysages qui toujours se renouvellent,
Des couchers de soleil miraculeux, des villes
Pleines de palais blancs, de ponts, de campaniles
Et de lumières scintillantes... Des visages
Très beaux, très gais; des danses
Comme dans ces ballets auxquels je pense,
Interprétés par Jean Borlin. Je veux des plages
Au décor de féerie,
Avec des étrangers sportifs aux noms de princes
Des étrangères en souliers de pierreries
Et de splendides chiens neigeux aux jambes minces.

Je veux, frôlés de Rolls silencieuses,
De longs trottoirs de velours blond. Terrasses,
Orchestres bourdonnant de musiques heureuses...
Vois-tu, Filliou, le Carnaval qui passe?
La Riviéra débordante de roses?
J'ai besoin de ne voir un instant que ces choses
Quand je serai guérie!

J'aurai ce châle aux éclatantes broderies
Qui fait songer aux courses espagnoles,
Des cheveux courts en auréole
Comme Maë Murray, des yeux qui rient,
Un teint de cuivre et l'air, non pas d'être guérie,
Mais de n'avoir jamais connu de maladie!

Once I've Been Cured

Once I've been cured, Filliou,
I'll want to see nothing but pretty things...

Luxurious flowers in endless blossomings,
Landscapes forever fresh and new,
Sunsets miraculous, bell-towers, white
Palaces, bridges, sparkling in the light...
Beautiful faces, bright and gay,
Dancers I only dream about today—
Like Jean Borlin leaping his *entrechats*...
And oh, the beaches!... Ah,
Yes! That's what I'm going to long to see,
Beaches graced with a fairy touch,
And muscled strangers—Princes Such-and-Such—
Ladies with jeweled slippers, finery,
Splendid dogs, lean of leg and white as snow...

I'll want long promenades, plush and blond, where,
With voices hushed, Rolls Royces come and go.
Terraces, orchestras abuzz with their
Beautiful music... Carnaval, Filliou!
The rose-strewn Côte d'Azur... See?... Rest assured,
One glance is all I'll need! Just one will do,
For me to see those lovely things,
Once I've been cured! •

I'll wear that brilliant-spangled cape that brings
To mind a rash torero, and my hair
Will halo round my head, Mae Murray style,
Cut short. My eyes will wear a twinkling smile,
My fair skin will be bronze-tinged, with an air
Of health, without an inkling anywhere
Of that cruel illness that stalked me a while!

J'aurai tous les parfums, "les plus rares qui soient",
Une chambre moderne aux nuances hardies,
Une piscine rouge et des coussins de soie
Un peu cubistes. J'ai besoin de fantaisie...

J'ai besoin de sorbets et de liqueurs glacées,
De fruits craquants, de raisins doux, d'amandes fraîches.
Peut-être d'ambroisie...
Ou simplement de mordre au coeur neuf d'une pêche?

J'ai besoin d'oublier tant de sombres pensées,
Tant de bols de tisane et d'heures accablantes!
Il me faudra, vois-tu, des choses si vivantes
Et si belles, Filliou... si belles—ou si gaies!

Nul ne sait à quel point nous sommes fatiguées,
Toutes deux, de ce gris de la tapisserie,
De l'armoire immobile et de ces noires baies
Que le laurier nous tend derrière la fenêtre.

Tant de voyages, dis, de pays à connaître,
De choses qu'on rêvait, qui pourront être
Quand je serai guérie...

I'll have perfumes, "the rarest one can buy".
A room with brash motifs, a red-tiled pool,
Cushions of silk with cubist shapes. For I
Yearn for a life where fantasy's the rule...

I'll yearn for sorbets, iced liqueurs, and cool
Almonds, crisp fruit, grapes succulent and sweet.
Ambrosia too, perhaps, to eat?
Or simply sink my teeth into a peach?

I'll yearn to cast out somber thoughts, forget
All those depressing moments, banish each
And every hot *tisane!* I'll want to let
Nothing but living things into my life:
Beautiful, happy, living things, Filliou!

For no one knows how tired we are, we two,
Of those gray-papered walls, dull furniture,
The laurel-berries, black, beyond the sill.

So many countries, travels, pleasure-rife,
Dreams only dreamt, that soon I will fulfill
Once I've been cured...

LAST PAGES
FROM SABINE'S NOTEBOOK

La main des dieux, tu peux refuser de la prendre.
La main du mendiant, tu peux aussi.
Toutes les mains qui frôleront la tienne, tu peux les oublier.
La main de ton ami, ferme les doigts sur elle, et serre-la si
fort que le sang de ton coeur y batte avec le sien au même
  rythme.

   • • •

Tu te chaufferas au feu de paysan?
Je me chaufferai au feu de paysan.
Tu auras de vieilles lampes à pétrole?
Je les aurai.
Un jardin de curé?
Un jardin de curé.
Et un pot de basilic?
Et deux pots de basilic.
Et ta pitié pour moi et ma pitié pour toi.

   • • •

N'oublie pas la chanson du soleil, Vassili.
Elle est dans les chemins craquelés de l'été,
dans la paille des meules,
dans le bois sec de ton armoire
...si tu sais bien l'entendre.
Elle est aussi dans le coeur du criquet.
Vassili, Vassili, parce que tu as froid, ce soir,
Ne nie pas le soleil.

   • • •

Hand of the gods... You can refuse to take it.
Hand of the beggars... You can do the same.
All the hands that might graze your own, you can ignore.
But your friend's hand... Ah! Clutch it round, squeeze it so
    tight
that your heart pounds its blood with his in one same beat.

                    • • •

Will you warm yourself by a peasant fire?
I'll warm myself by a peasant fire.
Will you have old petrol lamps for light?
I'll have them too.
A parish priest's garden?
A parish priest's garden.
And a pot of basil?
And two pots of basil.
And your pity for me and my pity for you.

                    • • •

Don't forget what the sun is singing, Vassili.
Its song is in the summer's crackling paths,
in the stack of straw,
in the dry wood piling up in your shed,
...if you know how to hear it.
It's in the cricket's heart as well.
Vassili, Vassili, just because you're cold tonight,
Don't say there is no sun.

                    • • •

Ne regarde pas si loin, Vassili, tu me fais peur.
N'est-il pas assez grand le cirque des steppes?
Le ciel s'ajuste au bord.
Ne laisse pas ton âme s'échapper au delà comme un cheval
    sauvage.
Tu vois comme je suis perdue dans l'herbe.
J'ai besoin que tu me regardes, Vassili.

            • • •

Ne parle pas d'absence, toi qui ne sais pas.
Mets seulement ta joue contre la mienne.
As-tu jamais interrogé la porte qui doit s'ouvrir pour le retour
et désespéré...?
As-tu jamais, au petit jour, songé qu'on pourrait
ne plus se revoir peut-être et imaginé?...
Serre-moi plus fort.
Nos deux ombres séparées, que deviendraient-elles?

            • • •

La chaise vide... Ah comment feras-tu
pour supporter cela?
Et moi qui pars, comment ferai-je
pour supporter le reste?

Don't gaze so far off, Vassili, you frighten me.
Isn't the circus of the steppes big enough?
The sky comes settling in on their edge.
Don't let your soul, like a wild horse, run free.
You know how lost I am here in the grass.
I need you to gaze on me, Vassili.

· · ·

Don't talk about absence, you who have no notion.
Just lay your cheek against mine, here.
A door about to open... Did you ever, hopeless,
ask it who was returning?...
Did you ever think, at dawn's first light, that you and I
might never again see each other, ever dream it?...
Hold me, hug me tighter, tighter...
What would our shadows be, each one, without the other?

· · ·

The empty chair... Ah! what will you do
to bear such a thing?
And I, who am leaving, what will I do
to bear all the rest?

NOTES

THE LITTLE MUSHROOM

"Petit Poucet" or Tom Thumb (strophe 7) is a reference to the well-known Perrault tale, where the youngest and smallest of seven brothers manages to defeat an ogre and save his family by using his wits.

FAFOU

The unsettling mood of the poem reflects the influence of French poet Maurice Rollinat (1846-1903), a master of the macabre. This poem established the authenticity of Sabine's poetry (see Introduction).

"Yatagan" (strophe 3) is a Turkish saber with a curved blade.

THE GRAPE LEFT BEHIND

Here Sabine does not differentiate between the masculine "le grain" (the grape) and the feminine "la graine" (the seed), and she interchanges them freely. Since these two words are not similar in English, we chose to keep the word "grape" throughout.

THE LABURNUM

"The Laburnum" and "Autumn Morning" were both presented to the Jeux Floraux de France in 1925. The Jeux Floraux is probably the oldest poetry contest in the world. It was first organized in the fourteenth century by seven rich troubadours from Toulouse and has kept the tradition ever since. The winners of the contest receive a gold or a silver flower (hence the name of the contest). Poets Jean Richepin and Anna de Noailles presided over the 1925 Jeux Floraux, where Sabine received the Grand Prize for "Autumn Morning" and another prize for "The Laburnum."

THE GOAT

The reference (strophe 6) is to the well-known story "La Chèvre de Monsieur Seguin," one of the *Lettres de mon moulin* (1869) by popular novelist Alphonse Daudet, in which a foolhardy *provençale* goat, yearning for the freedom of the mountain, comes to grief despite her courageous battle against the wolf.

THE HEATHER

"Côte d'Argent" is the coast between Arcachon and Biarritz in the southwestern region of France.

THE PILGRIMS OF THE DUNE

"Les chanteurs de l'Ukraine" or Ukrainian singers (strophe 5) have long been celebrated for their unusually deep and rich *basso profundo*.

THE LA RHUNE FUNICULAR

La Rhune is a Basque country mountain on the Spanish border.

"Quebranta" refers to Don Quebranta Huesos, whose name in Spanish suggests "bone-crusher", and one version of whose story appeared in "Don Quebranta Huesos: a Tale of Southern Spain", by E. and H. Heron (pseud. Hesketh V. Prichard and Kate O'Brien Ryall Prichard), in *The Badminton Magazine,* January 1898. The hero tells us at the outset that the events he is about to recount occurred upon a mountain range within sight of two continents, hence Sabine's allusion.

LA SOLITUDE

"Les bêtes à Bon Dieu"—God's bugs—(strophe 2) is a colloquial French name for *coccinelles* or ladybugs.

"The Donkey and the Horse" (strophe 5) is the title of one of Aesop's fables.

FIRST LEAVES

"Cassandra-voiced" (strophe 3): Cassandra was the daughter of Priam, king of Troy. She was condemned by Apollo to prophesy correctly—especially disasters—but never to be believed. Here the walls forewarn the young leaves of the many dangers they will encounter, but the leaves choose not to believe them.

THE TREES' PATH

The Young Elm's Path: *Autan* is a name for a stormy wind blowing toward Toulouse along the Garonne valley (strophe 3).

The Reed's Path: a reference to La Fontaine's well-known fable, "The Oak and the Reed", in which the reed tells the oak "I bend but never break." Indeed, the next storm uproots the oak, but leaves the reed untouched. Sabine, like many of La Fontaine's successors, enjoyed toying with the moral.

"I didn't happen on the baobab" (last line of the poem): The exoticism and sonorous name of the baobab—the spreading tree with its twisting limbs, common to West Africa—contribute to its popularity among children. Sabine humorously ends her poem with a tongue-in-cheek allusion, since everyone knows that she could not have met the baobab anyway. Later, in 1943, Antoine de Saint-Exupéry famously referred to the baobab in *The Little Prince*.

AUTUMN'S CREEPING VINE

The French *vigne vierge* is usually translated as "Virginia Creeper," which would not be very appropriate here. I would have liked to keep the notion of "vierge", given the context, but have had to settle for the present compromise. Note too the very free rhymes and meters, similar to Sabine's—*Trans*.

THE PLANE TREE HOUR

"Cordoue" or Cordoba (strophe 3): The well-known Moorish city in southern Spain is famous for the quality of its leathers.

THE OLD WOMAN IN THE MOON

The woman in the moon, young or old, is a common image in French folklore and in children's imagination. Further on, Sabine seems to refer to the biblical story of the man—changing him into a woman in accordance with the usual French feminization of the moon—who was punished by God for gathering firewood on the Sabbath. His identification is found in a number of folkloric and literary variations.

THE CINEMA

"A story line, a point or two." (strophe 3): A reference to the text placed between pictures in silent films.

Rimsky-Korsakov (strophe 8), as the composer of *Scheherazade,* is part of a fantasy world that includes tales from *A Thousand and One Nights,* Aladdin's gardens, and modern "magicians" such as Charlie Chaplin and Buster Keaton.

PEACE

Jean-Baptiste Corot, Pierre-Cécil Puvis de Chavannes, Eugène Carrière, and Henri Martin are all nineteenth-century landscape French painters. Martin, like Sabine, was from the Lot region (strophe 8).

HORSES' PATH

In the two-line strophes at the end of the poem Sabine repeats the words of a children's jump-rope song where horses of various colors are made to rhyme with the names of different cities. The last three lines of the poem return to the white horse of Sabine's dream.

WHEN I LIVED OFF IN FLORENCE

The idea of reincarnation, found in Buddhism, is particularly vivid in this poem, but it is also found in "Eastern Paths," "Western Paths," "Northland Paths" and "Southern Paths."

"Beatrice" (strophe 3): I would hope that "Beatrice" would be read with four syllables, and pronounced as in Italian. But even if anglicized it can be made to scan. Let the reader decide—*Trans.*

EASTERN PATHS

"Niania": name given to a Russian nanny; "baba": from *babooshka* (grandmother); "isba": Russian hut or log-house.

WESTERN PATHS

Popocatepetl: Highest volcano in Mexico. Tres Puntas: This could refer to one of two popular tourist resorts—Cerro Tres Puntas, a mountain in Chile, and Cabo Tres Puntas, in the Tortugas, north of Venezuela.

NORTHERN PATHS

This Nordic fantasy is, apparently, a testimony to Sabine's admiration for Swedish novelist Selma Lagerlöf (1858-1940), born in the village of Marbacka (last strophe), and for her often supernatural folkloric tales. The one specifically referred to, *The Wonderful Adventures of Nils Holgerson* (1906), recounts the travels of a mischievous child-turned-dwarf, who flies from Sweden to Lapland on the back of his farmyard goose.

"The name Vancouver turned me pale" (line 1) is a line from a poem published two years earlier in Belgium. Since its author, Marcel Thiry, was little known at the time, Sabine probably became acquainted with his work through a review published in a newspaper. Bernard Delvaille, in his preface to a 1975 publication of the complete works of Marcel Thiry, suggests that Sabine may have read an article by George Marlow, that appeared in the *Mercure de France.*

SOUTHERN PATHS

The reference to Ravel's "Bolero" leads us to believe that a line of this poem was altered by one of the editors because Ravel's work was first performed four months after Sabine's death. The Sicauds, like Ravel, spent some of their summer vacations in the Basque country, especially Ciboure, where Ravel was born, and they may have met there. This could explain the editors' decision to change a musical title that was either illegible or dated, and replace it with the famous "Bolero". A comparison between the publication by Louis Vaunois of three of Sabine's poems in 1945, and their publication by Millepierres in 1958 shows that minor changes were made on punctuation and paragraph formatting (for example, a dash rather than a semi-colon, a capital letter at the beginning of every line, an occasional different spacing between paragraphs, etc.). This may also be due to the difficulty of interpreting a handwritten text.

WIDOW'S PATH

Without following her liberties exactly, I have tried to preserve the effect of Sabine's unorthodox, even non-existent rhymes, in spite of (or perhaps because of) which her verse achieves a remarkable and simple musicality—*Trans.*

THE ROAD TO THE HIGH PLATEAUS

Pujols is a small town between Bordeaux and Villeneuve. In Villeneuve, the Tour de Pujols marks the beginning of the road leading to it.

THE CHATEAU DE BIRON

This chateau, located in the south of the Dordogne valley, has been the property of the Gontaut-Biron family since the 12th century. It was restored at the end of the 15th century in Italian Renaissance style (hence the reference to Italy in the poem) and then restored again in the 18th and 19th century. It is now open to visitors.

THE LEPERS' GROTTO

Gavaudun, in the southwestern part of France, is a tourist resort known for its picturesque gorges and grottoes.

THE GARDENS' PATH

It is very common for old French houses to have niches holding a statue of the Virgin Mary (strophe 4). Here, because the tree has been stripped of most of its limbs, it can no longer protect the statue from the elements.

DOCTORS

Bouchut (strophe 4) was Sabine's cat. He seemed instinctively to know which herbs would cure his minor ailments.

FEVER DAYS

Alcarazas (strophe 6) is an Arabic word for porous earthen vases, in which drinking water is kept cool through evaporation.

PAIN, I ABHOR YOU

L'Honneur de souffrir (Honor in Suffering) is a volume of poetry published in 1927 by Anna de Noailles (1876-1933). A year earlier, Noailles had written the preface to Sabine's *Childhood Poems*. Despite these two poets' common passion for nature, Noailles does not seem to have influenced Sabine's poetry. Sabine usually remains an observer of nature, and seems to disappear into her protagonists. Noailles, on the other hand, often projects herself upon nature. The difference is even greater in "the illness poems," where suffering is intellectualized in Noailles, but delivered with all its rawness in Sabine.

SPRING

This poem was first published by Louis Vaunois in 1945 under the title "Jour d'espoir."

In strophe 8, Sabine loosely quotes a line from "Le Passeur d'eau" [The Ferryman], a poem included in *Les Villages illusoires* [Illusory Villages] by Emile Verhaeren (1855-1916), where a boatman is seen rowing toward his death. "Le passeur d'eau, les mains aux rames / A contre flot, depuis longtemps, / Luttait, un roseau vert entre les dents." (The boatman, clutching at each oar, / Against the tide, long struggled toward the shore /

a tender reed between his teeth.) Here, Sabine also makes an indirect allusion to her own journey toward death.

ILLNESS

"Filliou" (line 1) was a term of endearment given to Madame Ginet-Sicaud by her mother. Sabine and her brother Claude often called her by this name.

Chamonix and Ciboure (strophe 4): Chamonix is a ski resort located near Mont Blanc in the French Alps. Ciboure is a small Basque coastal town adjacent to St Jean de Luz.

"Lotus's Heart and Stalk of Bamboo" (last strophe). The Buddhist-sounding title of this tale points to the Sicauds' lingering interest in Buddhism. Closely related to the water lily, the lotus is a sacred flower symbolizing creative power. Although it grows out of mud, the lotus's beauty remains untarnished, hence it also symbolizes the purity of the Buddha. The bamboo is connected with longevity and durability. Its elegant forms are frequently represented in Japanese and Chinese works of art.

ONCE I'VE BEEN CURED

Jean Borlin (strophe 2) was a ballet celebrity of the period, famous for his choreography of Cocteau's *Les Mariés de la Tour Eiffel,* which had premiered in 1921. He was one of many contemporary personalities immortalized in posters by the caricaturist Steinlen, which Sabine might well have seen.

After gaining fame as a dancer, beauty Mae Murray (strophe 4)—"The Girl with the Bee-Stung Lips"—went on to star in silent films opposite such leading men as John Gilbert and Rudolph Valentino. Unfortunately, her voice was not as pleasant as her looks, and the advent of the talkies gradually ended her career. Sabine's reference to her "short hair" is curious. She is usually pictured with rather full, wavy locks.

LAST PAGES

Vassili is Sabine's imaginary romantic friend.

BIBLIOGRAPHY

WORKS BY SABINE SICAUD

Poèmes d'enfant. Poitiers: Cahiers de France, 1926.

Les Poèmes de Sabine Sicaud. Ed. François Millepierres. Paris: Stock, 1958.

Sabine Sicaud: Le Rêve inachevé. Ed. Odile Ayral-Clause. Bordeaux: Les Dossiers d'Aquitaine, 1996.

Que nul ne vienne. Que ninguém venha. Trans. Maria da Luz Miranda, Lisbon: Edições Fluviais, 2002. (French and Portuguese bilingual edition of selected poems.)

ANTHOLOGIES

Bealu, Marcel. *Anthologie de la poésie féminine française de 1900 à nos jours.* Paris: Stock, 1953.

Gossez, A-M. *Les Poètes du vingtième siècle.* Paris: Eugène Figuière, 1929.

Moulin, Jeanine. *La Poésie féminine.* 2 vols. Paris: Seghers, 1963-66.

Sabatier, Robert. *La Poésie du vingtième siècle.* 3 vols. Paris: Albin Michel, 1982.

Seghers, Pierre. *Livre d'Or de la poésie française.* 2 vols. Verviers, Belgium: Marabout Université, 1961-69.

Shapiro, Norman R. *French Women Poets of Nine Centuries: The Distaff and the Pen.* Baltimore: John Hopkins University Press, 2008.

Siraux, Y., P. Parre and A. Bouyer. *Anthologie de la poésie française.* Namur: Wesmsel-Charlier, 1961.

Vaunois, Louis and Jacques Bour. *Les Poètes de la vie.* Paris: Corréa, 1945.

Walch, Gérard and Pascal Bonetti, *Anthologie des poètes français contemporains.* 5 vols. Paris: Delagrave, 1958.

GENERAL WORKS

Clancier, Georges Emmanuel. *Littérature française.* 2 vols. Paris: Larousse, 1972.

Clouard, Henri. *Histoire de la littérature française du symbolisme à nos jours*. Paris: Albin Michel, 1949.

Moulin, Jeanine. *Huit siècles de poésie féminine*. Paris: Seghers, 1975.

Taillardas, Jean-Paul. *Le Portail de la Solitude*. Paris, 1986.

Thiry, Marcel. *Toi qui pâlis au nom de Vancouver. Oeuvres poétiques (1924-1974)*. Paris: Seghers, 1975.

Vandromme, Pol. *Dictionnaire de la littérature contemporaine*. Paris: Editions Universitaires, 1962.

ARTICLES

Adam, Pierre. "Dix minutes avec une petite fille qui écrit des chefs-d'œuvre," *La Petite Gironde*, 8 July 1925.

Ayral-Clause, Odile. "Espoir et souffrance dans la poésie de Sabine Sicaud." *Selecta* 9 (1988), pp. 23-29.

Bonnat, René. "Sabine Sicaud," *Revue de l'Agenais*, 1926, p. 414.

Celli, Rose. "Sabine Sicaud," *Cahiers du Sud* 19-218, July 1939, pp. 553-56.

Dufaur, Marguerite. "Sabine Sicaud enfant et poète de génie." *La Dépêche*, 26 April-3 May 1953.

Fechner, Marguerite. "Lettre à Maurice Luxembourg." *Revue de l'Agenais*, 1974, pp. 415-29.

Jeanier, Gabrielle. " Sabine Sicaud l'enfant poète," *Atlantica*, 62 (March 1999).

Jeantin, Paul. "'Le Petit Cèpe' a cinquante ans." *Revue de l'Agenais*, 1974, pp. 415-429.

——. "Une Ame d'enfant... un grand poète." *Bibliothèque Municipale d'Agen*, 1978, pp. 1-18.

Millepierres, François, "Commentaires," *Combat-Lettres*, 13 Nov. 1958.

Noailles, Anna de. "Sabine Sicaud," *Le Quotidien*, 22 July 1928.

Prevost, Marcel, "Discours officiel du Jasmin d'argent de
     1924." *Revue du Jasmin d'argent,* 1924, pp. 34–38.
Rézelin, Juliette. "Sabine Sicaud," *Les Cahiers de l'Etoile.* Vol. 5,
     Sept.–Oct. 1928, pp. 567–72.
"Sabine Sicaud." *Sud-Ouest,* 24 Apr. 1997.
Toesca, Maurice, "Sabine Sicaud: Poésies posthumes," *Figaro
     Madame,* 15 Apr. 1987.

EXHIBITION

"Sabine Sicaud: 1913-1928." Bibliothèque municipale d'Agen,
     27 Nov.–31 Dec. 1978.

AUTHORS' BIOGRAPHIES

Norman R. Shapiro, honored as one of the leading contemporary translators of French, holds a B.A., M.A., and Ph.D. from Harvard University and, as Fulbright scholar, the Diplome de Langue et Lettres Francaises from the Universite d'Aix-Marseille. He is Professor of Romance Languages and Literatures at Wesleyan University and is currently Writer in Residence at Adams House at Harvard University. His published volumes span the centuries, medieval to modern, and the genres: poetry, novel, and theater. Among them are *Four Farces by Georges Feydeau; The Comedy of Eros: Medieval French Guides to the Art of Love; Selected Poems from Baudelaire's 'Les Fleurs du Mal'; One Hundred and One Poems of Paul Verlaine* (recipient of the MLA Scaglione Award); *Negritude: Black Poetry from Africa and the Caribbean;* and *Creole Echoes: The Francophone Poetry of Nineteenth-Century Louisiana.* A specialist in French fable literature, he has also published *Fables from Old French: Aesop's Beasts and Bumpkins* and *The Fabulists French: Verse Fables of Nine Centuries.* His definitive translations of La Fontaine, *The Complete Fables of Jean de la Fontaine,* was awarded the American Translators Association's prestigious Lewis Galantiere Prize for 2008. Recent and forthcoming titles include *French Women Poets of Nine Centuries: The Distaff and the Pen; Preversities: A Jacques Prevert Sampler;* and a newly re-illustrated edition of *La Fontaine's Bawdy.* Shapiro is a member of the Academy of American Poets.

Odile Ayral-Clause holds a Ph.D in French Literature from the University of Colorado, Boulder. Her paternal grandmother was born in the French region that nourished Sabine's poetic talents, and Ayral-Clause has devoted much of her career to bringing the work of this long-neglected *enfant prodige* to light. She interviewed the last persons to have known the Sicaud family about Sabine's brief and tragic career. Among several articles, her writings on Sicaud include the book, *Sabine Sicaud, le reve inacheve,* which was published in 1996 in France and gave rise to this present collection. Her most recent book is the widely acclaimed *Camille Claudel: A Life.* She teaches French at California Polytechnic State University, San Luis Obispo.

TITLES FROM BLACK WIDOW PRESS

TRANSLATION SERIES

Chanson Dada: Selected Poems by Tristan Tzara
Translated with an introduction and essay by Lee Harwood.

Approximate Man and Other Writings by Tristan Tzara
Translated and edited by Mary Ann Caws.

Poems of André Breton: A Bilingual Anthology
Translated with essays by Jean-Pierre Cauvin and Mary Ann Caws.

Last Love Poems of Paul Eluard
Translated with an introduction by Marilyn Kallet.

Capital of Pain by Paul Eluard
Translated by Mary Ann Caws, Patricia Terry, and Nancy Kline.

Love, Poetry (L'amour la poésie) by Paul Eluard
Translated with an essay by Stuart Kendall.

The Sea and Other Poems by Guillevic
Translated by Patricia Terry. Introduction by Monique Chefdor.

Essential Poems and Writings of Robert Desnos: A Bilingual Anthology
Edited with an introduction and essay by Mary Ann Caws.

Essential Poems and Writings of Joyce Mansour: A Bilingual Anthology
Translated with an introduction by Serge Gavronsky.

Poems of A. O. Barnabooth by Valery Larbaud
Translated by Ron Padgett and Bill Zavatsky.

EyeSeas (Les Ziaux) by Raymond Queneau
Translated with an introduction by Daniela Hurezanu and Stephen Kessler.

To Speak, to Tell You by Sabine Sicaud
Translated by Norman R. Shapiro. Introduction and notes by Odile Ayral-Clause.

Art Poétique by Guillevic *(Forthcoming)*
Translated by Maureen Smith.

Furor and Mystery and Other Writings by René Char *(Forthcoming)*
Edited and translated by Mary Ann Caws and Nancy Kline.

La Fontaine's Bawdy by Jean de la Fontaine *(Forthcoming)*
Translated with an introduction by Norman R. Shapiro.

Inventor of Love & Other Writings by Ghérasim Luca *(Forthcoming)*
Translated by Julian and Laura Semilian. Introduction by Andrei Codrescu. Essay by Petre Răileanu.

The Big Game by Benjamin Péret *(Forthcoming)*
Translated with an introduction by Marilyn Kallet.

I Want No Part in It and Other Writings by Benjamin Péret
Translated with an introduction by James Brook. *(Forthcoming)*

Essential Poems and Writings of Jules Laforgue *(Forthcoming)*
Translated and edited by Patricia Terry.

Preversities: A Jacques Prevert Sampler *(Forthcoming)*
Translated and edited by Norman R. Shapiro.

MODERN POETRY SERIES

An Alchemist with One Eye on Fire by Clayton Eshleman

Archaic Design by Clayton Eshleman

Backscatter: New and Selected Poems by John Olson

Crusader-Woman by Ruxandra Cesereanu
Translated by Adam J. Sorkin. Introduction by Andrei Codrescu.

The Grindstone of Rapport: A Clayton Eshleman Reader
Forty years of poetry, prose, and translations by Clayton Eshleman.

Packing Light: New and Selected Poems by Marilyn Kallet

Forgiven Submarine by Ruxandra Cesereanu and Andrei Codrescu
(Forthcoming)

Caveat Onus by Dave Brinks *(Forthcoming)*
Complete cycle, four volumes combined.

Fire Exit by Robert Kelly *(Forthcoming)*

NEW POETS SERIES

Signal from Draco: New and Selected Poems by Mebane Robertson

LITERARY THEORY/BIOGRAPHY SERIES

Revolution of the Mind: The Life of André Breton by Mark Polizzotti
Revised and augmented edition. *(Forthcoming)*

WWW.BLACKWIDOWPRESS.COM